www.EffortlessMath.com

... So Much More Online!

- ✓ FREE Math lessons
- ✓ More Math learning books!
- ✓ Mathematics Worksheets
- ✓ Online Math Tutors

Need a PDF version of this book?

Send email to: Info@EffortlessMath.com

5 Full-Length ISEE Middle Level Math Practice Tests

The Practice You Need to Ace the ISEE Middle Level Math Test

By

Reza Nazari & Ava Ross

All inquiries should be addressed to:

info@EffortlessMath.com

www.EffortlessMath.com

ISBN–13: 978-1-64612-139-7

ISBN–10: 1-64612-139-2

Published by: Effortless Math Education

www.EffortlessMath.com

Description

5 Full-Length ISEE Middle Level Math Practice Tests, which reflects the 2019 and 2020 test guidelines and topics, is designed to help you hone your math skills, overcome your exam anxiety, and boost your confidence -- and do your best to ace the ISEE Middle Level Math Test. The realistic and full-length ISEE Middle Level Math tests show you how the test is structured and what math topics you need to master. The practice test questions are followed by answer explanations to help you find your weak areas, learn from your mistakes, and raise your ISEE Middle Level Math score.

The surest way to succeed on ISEE Middle Level Math Test is with intensive practice in every math topic tested-- and that's what you will get in ***5 Full-Length ISEE Middle Level Math Practice Tests***. This ISEE Middle Level Math new edition has been updated to replicate questions appearing on the most recent ISEE Middle Level Math tests. This is a precious learning tool for ISEE Middle Level test takers who need extra practice in math to improve their ISEE Middle Level Math score. After taking the ISEE Middle Level Math practice tests in this book, you will have solid foundation and adequate practice that is necessary to succeed on the ISEE Middle Level Math test. **This book is your ticket to ace the ISEE Middle Level Math Test!**

5 Full-Length ISEE Middle Level Math Practice Tests contains many exciting and unique features to help you improve your test scores, including:

- Content 100% aligned with the 2019 - 2020 ISEE Middle Level Math test
- Written by ISEE Math tutors and test experts
- Complete coverage of all ISEE Middle Level Math concepts and topics which you will be tested
- Detailed answers and explanations for every ISEE Middle Level Math practice questions to help you learn from your mistakes
- 5 full-length practice tests (featuring new question types) with detailed answers

This ISEE Middle Level Math book and other Effortless Math Education books are used by thousands of students each year to help them review core content areas, brush-up in math, discover their strengths and weaknesses, and achieve their best scores on the ISEE Middle Level Math test.

About the Author

Reza Nazari is the author of more than 100 Math learning books including:
– **Math and Critical Thinking Challenges:** For the Middle and High School Student
– **GRE Math in 30 Days**
– **ASVAB Math Workbook 2018 - 2019**
– **Effortless Math Education Workbooks**
– **and many more Mathematics books ...**

Reza is also an experienced Math instructor and a test–prep expert who has been tutoring students since 2008. Reza is the founder of Effortless Math Education, a tutoring company that has helped many students raise their standardized test scores—and attend the colleges of their dreams. Reza provides an individualized custom learning plan and the personalized attention that makes a difference in how students view math.

You can contact Reza via email at:
reza@EffortlessMath.com

Find Reza's professional profile at:
goo.gl/zoC9rJ

Contents

Description 4
ISEE Middle Level Test Review 7
ISEE Middle Level Math Practice Test 1 9
ISEE Middle Level Math Practice Test 2 30
ISEE Middle Level Math Practice Test 3 51
ISEE Middle Level Math Practice Test 4 71
ISEE Middle Level Math Practice Test 5 92
ISEE Middle Level Math Practice Tests Answers and Explanations 113

ISEE Middle Level Test Review

The Independent School Entrance Exam (ISEE) is an admission test developed by the Educational Records Bureau for its member schools as part of their admission process.

ISEE Middle Level tests use a multiple-choice format and contain two Mathematics sections:

Quantitative Reasoning

There are 37 questions in the Quantitative Reasoning section and students have 35 minutes to answer the questions. This section contains word problems and quantitative comparisons. The word problems require either no calculation or simple calculation. The quantitative comparison items present two quantities, (A) and (B), and the student needs to select one of the following four answer choices:

(A) The quantity in Column A is greater.

(B) The quantity in Column B is greater.

(C) The two quantities are equal.

(D) The relationship cannot be determined from the information given.

Mathematics Achievement

There are 47 questions in the Mathematics Achievement section and students have 40 minutes to answer the questions. Mathematics Achievement measures students' knowledge of Mathematics requiring one or more steps in calculating the answer.

In this book, there are five complete ISEE Middle Level Quantitative Reasoning and Mathematics Achievement practice tests. Take these tests to see what score you'll be able to receive on a real ISEE Lower Level test.

Good luck!

Time to refine your skill with a practice examination

Take practice ISEE Middle Level Math Tests to simulate the test day experience. After you've finished, score your tests using the answer keys.

Before You Start

- You'll need a pencil and a timer to take the test.
- After you've finished the test, review the answer key to see where you went wrong.
- Use the answer sheet provided to record your answers. (You can cut it out or photocopy it)
- Students receive 1 point for every correct answer. There is no penalty for wrong or skipped questions.

Calculators are NOT permitted for the ISEE Middle Level Test

Good Luck!

ISEE Middle Level Math Practice Test 1

2019 - 2020

Two Parts

Total number of questions: 84

Part 1 (Quantitative Reasoning): 37 questions

Part 2 (Mathematics Achievement): 47 questions

Total time for two parts: 75 Minutes

ISEE Middle Level Practice Test Answer Sheets

Remove (or photocopy) this answer sheet and use it to complete the practice test.

ISEE Middle Level Practice Test 1

Quantitative Reasoning

1	Ⓐ Ⓑ Ⓒ Ⓓ	25	Ⓐ Ⓑ Ⓒ Ⓓ
2	Ⓐ Ⓑ Ⓒ Ⓓ	26	Ⓐ Ⓑ Ⓒ Ⓓ
3	Ⓐ Ⓑ Ⓒ Ⓓ	27	Ⓐ Ⓑ Ⓒ Ⓓ
4	Ⓐ Ⓑ Ⓒ Ⓓ	28	Ⓐ Ⓑ Ⓒ Ⓓ
5	Ⓐ Ⓑ Ⓒ Ⓓ	29	Ⓐ Ⓑ Ⓒ Ⓓ
6	Ⓐ Ⓑ Ⓒ Ⓓ	30	Ⓐ Ⓑ Ⓒ Ⓓ
7	Ⓐ Ⓑ Ⓒ Ⓓ	31	Ⓐ Ⓑ Ⓒ Ⓓ
8	Ⓐ Ⓑ Ⓒ Ⓓ	32	Ⓐ Ⓑ Ⓒ Ⓓ
9	Ⓐ Ⓑ Ⓒ Ⓓ	33	Ⓐ Ⓑ Ⓒ Ⓓ
10	Ⓐ Ⓑ Ⓒ Ⓓ	34	Ⓐ Ⓑ Ⓒ Ⓓ
11	Ⓐ Ⓑ Ⓒ Ⓓ	35	Ⓐ Ⓑ Ⓒ Ⓓ
12	Ⓐ Ⓑ Ⓒ Ⓓ	36	Ⓐ Ⓑ Ⓒ Ⓓ
13	Ⓐ Ⓑ Ⓒ Ⓓ	37	Ⓐ Ⓑ Ⓒ Ⓓ
14	Ⓐ Ⓑ Ⓒ Ⓓ		
15	Ⓐ Ⓑ Ⓒ Ⓓ		
16	Ⓐ Ⓑ Ⓒ Ⓓ		
17	Ⓐ Ⓑ Ⓒ Ⓓ		
18	Ⓐ Ⓑ Ⓒ Ⓓ		
19	Ⓐ Ⓑ Ⓒ Ⓓ		
20	Ⓐ Ⓑ Ⓒ Ⓓ		
21	Ⓐ Ⓑ Ⓒ Ⓓ		
22	Ⓐ Ⓑ Ⓒ Ⓓ		
23	Ⓐ Ⓑ Ⓒ Ⓓ		
24	Ⓐ Ⓑ Ⓒ Ⓓ		

Mathematics Achievement

1	Ⓐ Ⓑ Ⓒ Ⓓ	25	Ⓐ Ⓑ Ⓒ Ⓓ
2	Ⓐ Ⓑ Ⓒ Ⓓ	26	Ⓐ Ⓑ Ⓒ Ⓓ
3	Ⓐ Ⓑ Ⓒ Ⓓ	27	Ⓐ Ⓑ Ⓒ Ⓓ
4	Ⓐ Ⓑ Ⓒ Ⓓ	28	Ⓐ Ⓑ Ⓒ Ⓓ
5	Ⓐ Ⓑ Ⓒ Ⓓ	29	Ⓐ Ⓑ Ⓒ Ⓓ
6	Ⓐ Ⓑ Ⓒ Ⓓ	30	Ⓐ Ⓑ Ⓒ Ⓓ
7	Ⓐ Ⓑ Ⓒ Ⓓ	31	Ⓐ Ⓑ Ⓒ Ⓓ
8	Ⓐ Ⓑ Ⓒ Ⓓ	32	Ⓐ Ⓑ Ⓒ Ⓓ
9	Ⓐ Ⓑ Ⓒ Ⓓ	33	Ⓐ Ⓑ Ⓒ Ⓓ
10	Ⓐ Ⓑ Ⓒ Ⓓ	34	Ⓐ Ⓑ Ⓒ Ⓓ
11	Ⓐ Ⓑ Ⓒ Ⓓ	35	Ⓐ Ⓑ Ⓒ Ⓓ
12	Ⓐ Ⓑ Ⓒ Ⓓ	36	Ⓐ Ⓑ Ⓒ Ⓓ
13	Ⓐ Ⓑ Ⓒ Ⓓ	37	Ⓐ Ⓑ Ⓒ Ⓓ
14	Ⓐ Ⓑ Ⓒ Ⓓ	38	Ⓐ Ⓑ Ⓒ Ⓓ
15	Ⓐ Ⓑ Ⓒ Ⓓ	39	Ⓐ Ⓑ Ⓒ Ⓓ
16	Ⓐ Ⓑ Ⓒ Ⓓ	40	Ⓐ Ⓑ Ⓒ Ⓓ
17	Ⓐ Ⓑ Ⓒ Ⓓ	41	Ⓐ Ⓑ Ⓒ Ⓓ
18	Ⓐ Ⓑ Ⓒ Ⓓ	42	Ⓐ Ⓑ Ⓒ Ⓓ
19	Ⓐ Ⓑ Ⓒ Ⓓ	43	Ⓐ Ⓑ Ⓒ Ⓓ
20	Ⓐ Ⓑ Ⓒ Ⓓ	44	Ⓐ Ⓑ Ⓒ Ⓓ
21	Ⓐ Ⓑ Ⓒ Ⓓ	45	Ⓐ Ⓑ Ⓒ Ⓓ
22	Ⓐ Ⓑ Ⓒ Ⓓ	46	Ⓐ Ⓑ Ⓒ Ⓓ
23	Ⓐ Ⓑ Ⓒ Ⓓ	47	Ⓐ Ⓑ Ⓒ Ⓓ
24	Ⓐ Ⓑ Ⓒ Ⓓ		

ISEE Middle Level Math

Practice Test 1

Section 1

37 questions

Total time for this section: 35 Minutes

You may NOT use a calculator for this test.

1) Solve. $\frac{-50 \times 0.5}{5}$
A. -16
B. -5
C. 5
D. 16

2) A $\$41$ shirt now selling for $\$29$ is discounted by what percent?
A. 20%
B. 29%
C. 40%
D. 50%

3) $562{,}357{,}741 \times 0.0001$?
A. $562{,}357.741$
B. $56{,}235.7741$
C. $5{,}623.57741$
D. 562.357741

4) Jim purchased a table for 30% off and saved $\$24$. What was the original price of the table?
A. $\$80$
B. $\$110$
C. $\$115$
D. 150

5) If $f = 3x - 2y$ and $g = x + 5y$, what is $3f + g$?
A. $5x - y$
B. $5x - 2y$
C. $10x - 2y$
D. $10x - y$

6) Which of the following shows the numbers in increasing order?
A. $\frac{1}{7}, \frac{3}{5}, \frac{1}{3}, \frac{3}{4}$
B. $\frac{1}{7}, \frac{3}{5}, \frac{3}{4}, \frac{1}{3}$
C. $\frac{1}{7}, \frac{1}{3}, \frac{3}{5}, \frac{3}{4}$
D. $\frac{1}{7}, \frac{3}{4}, \frac{1}{3}, \frac{3}{5}$

7) What is the value of x in the following equation? $8^x = 512$
A. 2
B. 3
C. 4
D. 5

8) What is the value of x in the following figure?

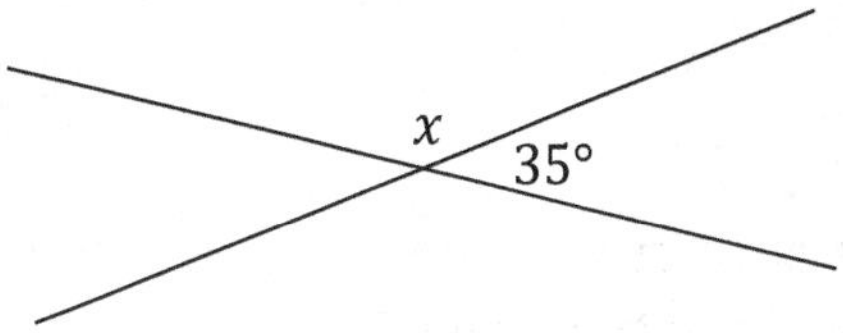

A. 35°
B. 75°
C. 115°
D. 145°

9) The score of Emma was half as that of Ava and the score of Mia was twice that of Ava. If the score of Mia was 40, what is the score of Emma?
A. 10
B. 18
C. 20
D. 30

10) The area of a circle is $49\ \pi$. What is the circumference of the circle?
A. 8π
B. 14π
C. 32π
D. 49π

11) Two third of 15 is equal to $\frac{5}{2}$ of what number?
A. 25
B. 15
C. 10
D. 4

12) What is round off the result of 1.15×8.2 to the nearest tenth?
A. 6
B. 7
C. 8.06
D. 9.4

13) The perimeter of the trapezoid below is 54. What is its area?

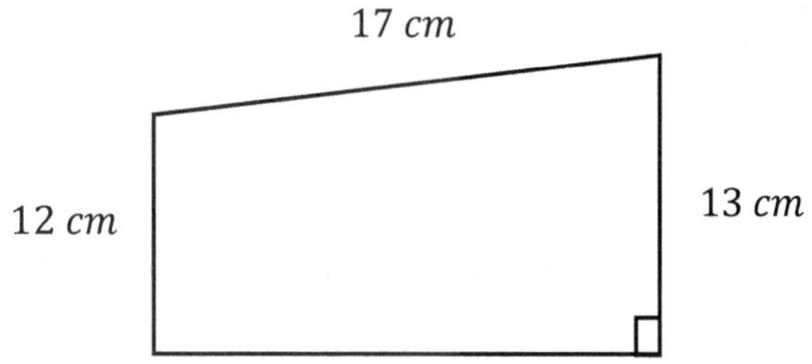

A. $255\ cm^2$
B. $234\ cm^2$
C. $150\ cm^2$
D. $100\ cm^2$

14) In five successive hours, a car traveled $42\ km$, $46\ km$, $52\ km$, $35\ km$ and $58\ km$. In the next five hours, it traveled with an average speed of $60\ km\ per\ hour$. Find the total distance the car traveled in 10 hours.

A. $435\ km$
B. $450\ km$
C. $475\ km$
D. $533\ km$

15) What is the mean in the following set of numbers?

$$10, 13, 29, 37, 46, 66, 100, 124$$

A. 46.2
B. 40.5
C. 51.4
D. 53.12

16) Find $\frac{1}{2}$ of $\frac{2}{5}$ of 145?

A. 30
B. 29
C. 18
D. 4

17) The price of a laptop is decreased by 20% to \$320. What is its original price?

A. \$320
B. \$380
C. \$400
D. \$455

18) A company pays its employee $\$7,500$ plus 3% of all sales profit. If x is all sold profit, which of the following represents the employee's revenue?

A. $0.03x$
B. $0.97x - 7,500$
C. $0.03x + 7,500$
D. $0.97x + 7,500$

19) The ratio of boys and girls in a class is $7:4$. If there are 44 students in the class, how many more girls should be enrolled to make the ratio $1:1$?

A. 8
B. 10
C. 12
D. 16

20) Which of the following is a correct statement?

A. $\frac{3}{5} > 0.8$
B. $12\% = \frac{2}{5}$
C. $3 < \frac{5}{2}$
D. $\frac{7}{6} > 0.8$

21) What is the value of x in the following equation?

$$6(x + 1) = 4(x - 4) + 20$$

A. 12
B. -12
C. 1
D. -1

22) What is the value of x in the following figure?

A. 160
B. 145
C. 125
D. 105

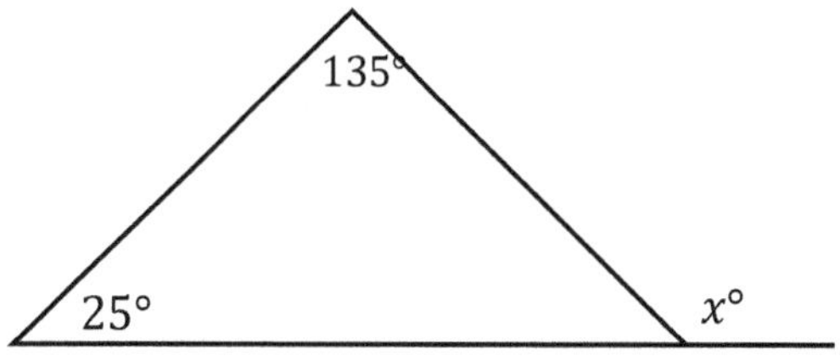

23) Car A use 4-liter petrol per 140 kilometers; car B use 3-liter petrol per 140 kilometers. If both cars drive 350 kilometers, how much more petrol does car A use?

A. 2.5
B. 10
C. 15.5
D. 25

24) What is the area of a square whose diagonal is 6?

A. 18
B. 32
C. 46
D. 64

25) What is value of $-25 - (-66)$?

A. 41
B. -91
C. -41
D. 91

Quantitative Comparisons

Direction: Questions 26 to 37 are Quantitative Comparisons Questions. Using the information provided in each question, compare the quantity in column A to the quantity in Column B. Choose on your answer sheet grid

A if the quantity in Column A is greater
B if the quantity in Column B is greater
C if the two quantities are equal
D if the relationship cannot be determined from the information given

26)

Column A	Column B
$\sqrt{36}+\sqrt{36}$	$\sqrt{72}$

27) $y=-4x-8$

Column A	Column B
The value of x when $y=12$	-4

28)

Column A	Column B
$6+4\times7+8$	$4+6\times7-8$

29) The average age of Joe, Michelle, and Nicole is 32.

Column A	Column B
The average age of Joe and Michelle	The average age of Michelle and Nicole

30)

Column A	**Column B**
$\sqrt{121-64}$	$\sqrt{121}-\sqrt{64}$

31) A right cylinder with radius 2 inches has volume 50π cubic inches.

Quantity A	Quantity B
The height of the cylinder	10 inches

32) x is an integer.

Quantity A	Quantity B
$\frac{x^6}{6}$	$(\frac{x}{6})^6$

33) x is an integer greater than zero.

Quantity A	Quantity B
$\frac{1}{x}+x$	8

34)

$$\frac{4}{5} < x < \frac{6}{7}$$

Quantity A	Quantity B
x	$\frac{5}{6}$

35) a and b are real numbers.

$$a < b$$

Quantity A	Quantity B
$\lvert a-b \rvert$	$\lvert b-a \rvert$

36) $2x^3 + 10 = 64$
$120 - 18y = 84$

Quantity A	Quantity B
x	y

37) The average of $3, 4$, and x is 3.

Quantity A	Quantity B
x	average of $x, x - 6, x + 4, 2x$

IF YOU FINISH BEFORE TIME IS CALLED, YOU MAY CHECK YOUR WORK ON THIS SECTION ONLY. DO NOT TURN TO OTHER SECTION IN THE TEST.

STOP

ISEE Middle Level Math

Practice Test 1

Section 2

47 questions

Total time for this section: 40 Minutes

You may NOT use a calculator for this test.

1) What number is 5 less than 50% of 46?
A. 10
B. 13
C. 18
D. 23

2) $4\left(\frac{1}{3}-\frac{1}{6}\right)+5$?
A. 4
B. 4.5
C. $5.66\ldots$
D. 5

3) What number is 15 more than 20% of 120?
A. 39
B. 29
C. 25
D. 20

4) In a bundle of 85 pencils, 42 are red and the rest are blue. About what percent of the bundle is composed of blue pencils?
A. 62%
B. 58%
C. 54%
D. 51%

5) What is the value of x in the following equation?

$$(x+6)^3 = 64$$

A. 1
B. -1
C. 2
D. -2

6) If a box contains red and blue balls in ratio of $3:2$, how many red balls are there if 90 blue balls are in the box?
A. 140
B. 135
C. 60
D. 10

7) What is the difference in perimeter between a $8\ cm$ by $5\ cm$ rectangle and a circle with diameter of $12\ cm$? $(\pi = 3)$

A. $8\ cm$
B. $9\ cm$
C. $10\ cm$
D. $11\ cm$

8) When a number is subtracted from 27 and the difference is divided by that number, the result is 2. What is the value of the number?

A. 2
B. 5
C. 9
D. 12

9) If $\frac{3x}{2} = 15$, then $\frac{2x}{5} = ?$

A. 4
B. 8
C. 10
D. 20

10) The price of a car was $\$20{,}000$ in 2014, and it was $\$15{,}000$ in 2015. What is the rate of depreciation of the price of car per year?

A. 15%
B. 25%
C. 30%
D. 35%

11) Which of the following is the greatest number?

A. $\frac{1}{4}$
B. $\frac{7}{9}$
C. 0.85
D. 75%

12) Calculate the approximate area of the following circle. (The diameter of the circle is 10 cm)

A. $1250\ cm^2$
B. $314 cm^2$
C. $116\ cm^2$
D. $78.5\ cm^2$

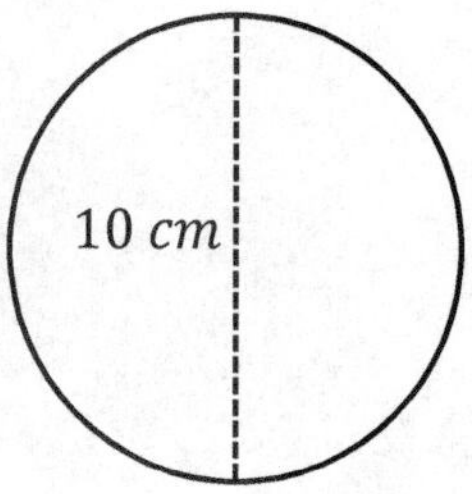

13) 90 is equal to?

A. $2 + (3 \times 10) + (2 \times 30)$
B. $\left(\frac{10}{3} \times 27\right) + (\frac{5}{2} \times 2)$
C. $(\left(\frac{3}{2} + 3\right) \times \frac{18}{3}) + 63$
D. $(2 \times 15) + (50 \times 2) - 46$

14) Which of the following angles can represent the three angles of an isosceles right triangle?

A. $45°, 90°, 45°$
B. $50°, 50°, 80°$
C. $60°, 60°, 60°$
D. $55°, 35°, 90°$

15) If 120% of a number is 84, then what is 90% of that number?

A. 45
B. 63
C. 74
D. 84

16) What is the missing term in the given numbers?

$$3, 4, 6, 9, 13, 18, 24, \_\_, 39$$

A. 24
B. 26
C. 27
D. 31

17) In following rectangle which statement is true?

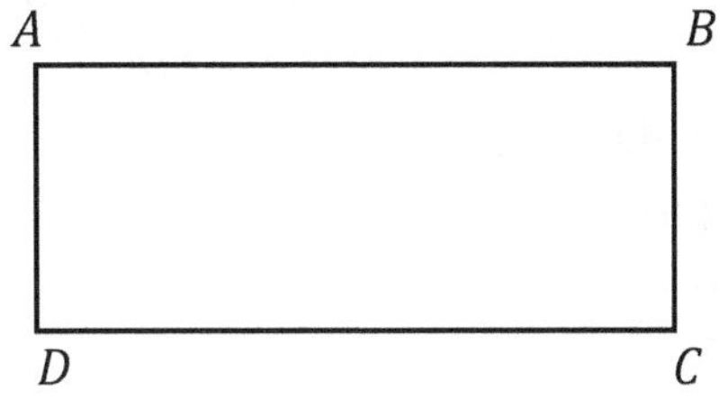

A. Length of AB is smaller than BC.
B. The sum of all the angles equals 360 degrees.
C. Length of AB equal to length DC.
D. AB is perpendicular to DC.

18) A football team had $\$25,000$ to spend on supplies. The team spent $\$15,000$ on new balls. New sport shoes cost $\$130$ each. Which of the following inequalities represent how many new shoes the team can purchase?

A. $130x + 15,000 \leq 25,000$
B. $130x + 15,000 \geq 25,000$
C. $15,000x + 130 \leq 25,000$
D. $15,000x + 130 \geq 25,000$

19) The capacity of a red box is 30% greater than a blue box. If the capacity of the red box is 52 books, how many books can be put in the blue box?

A. 9
B. 15
C. 40
D. 42

20) From last year, the price of gasoline has increased from $\$1.40$ per gallon to $\$1.75$ per gallon. The new price is what percent of the original price?

A. 72%
B. 125%
C. 140%
D. 160%

21) When a gas tank can hold 30 gallons, how many gallons does it contain when it is $\frac{2}{3}$ full?

A. 115
B. 65.5
C. 20
D. 10

22) 190 minutes = ...?

A. 3.25 *Hours*
B. 3.16 *Hours*
C. 2 *Hours*
D. 0.4 *Hours*

23) Which of the following is **NOT** a prime number?

A. 107
B. 101
C. 71
D. 58

24) What is the perimeter of a square that has an area of 36 square inches?
A. 144 inches
B. 36 inches
C. 24 inches
D. 56 inches

25) Jason left a $\$13.00$ tip on a lunch that cost $\$26.00$, what percentage was the tip?

A. 2.5%
B. 10%
C. 25%
D. 50%

26) A box of 36 pencils costs $1.80, what is the unit cost?
A. $\$0.50$
B. $\$0.25$
C. $\$0.08$
D. $\$0.05$

27) Two-kilograms apple and two-kilograms orange cost $\$26.4$ If one-kilogram apple costs $\$4.2$ how much does one-kilogram orange cost?
A. $\$9$
B. $\$6$
C. $\$4.5$
D. $\$4$

28) $[6 \times (-24) + 8] - (-4) + [6 \times 5] \div 2 \ = ?$
A. 158
B. 132
C. -104
D. -117

29) The width of a rectangle is $3x$ and its length is $5x$. The perimeter of the rectangle is 80. What is the value of x?
A. 4
B. 5
C. 6
D. 10

30) Jason is 15 miles ahead of Joe running at 5.5 miles per hour and Joe is running at the speed of 7 miles per hour. How long does it take Joe to catch Jason?

A. 4 hours
B. $6\ hours$
C. $8hours$
D. $10\ hours$

31) $\left(\left((-12) + 20\right) \times 3\right) + (-16)?$

A. 1
B. 4
C. 6
D. 8

32) If 45% of a class are girls, and 20% of girls play tennis, what percent of the class play tennis?

A. 9%
B. 15%
C. 25%
D. 40%

33) The price of a sofa is decreased by 30% to $\$490$. What was its original price?

A. $\$480$
B. $\$510$
C. $\$550$
D. $\$700$

34) In a class, there are twice as many girls as boys. If the total number of students in the class is 45, how many girls are in the class?

A. 15
B. 25
C. 32
D. 35

35) At a Zoo, the ratio of lions to tigers is 5 to 3. Which of the following could NOT be the total number of lions and tigers in the zoo?

A. 32
B. 40
C. 97
D. 104

36) Solving the equation: $10x - 15.5 = -55.5$?

A. -4
B. -3
C. 4
D. 3

37) A shaft rotates 400 times in 5 seconds. How many times does it rotate in 0.25 minutes?

A. $1{,}200$
B. 950
C. 400
D. 100

38) A swimming pool holds $2{,}500$ cubic feet of water. The swimming pool is 40 feet long and 10 feet wide. How deep is the swimming pool?

A. 6.25 feet
B. 12 feet
C. 40 feet
D. 100 feet

39) What is the value of x in the following equation?

$$6^x = 7{,}776$$

A. 3
B. 4
C. 5
D. 6

40) What is the value of x in the following equation?

$$10 + 5(x + 5 - 5x) = 40$$

A. -3
B. $-\frac{1}{4}$
C. $\frac{1}{4}$
D. 3

41) What is the area of the trapezoid?

A. 25
B. 45
C. 100
D. 150

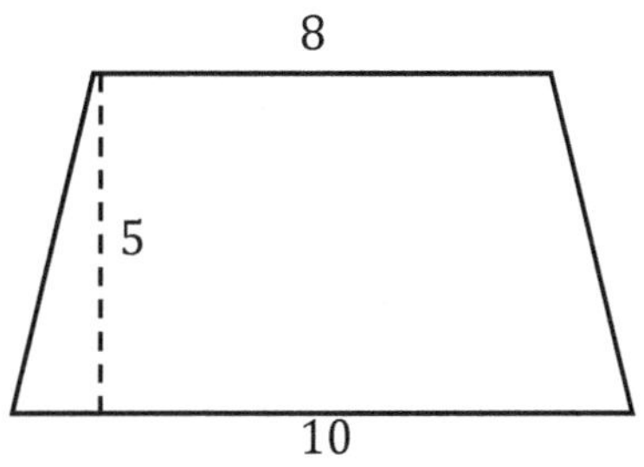

42) $13.125 \div 0.005$?

A. 2.625
B. 26.25
C. 262.5
D. 2,625

43) A card is drawn at random from a standard 52–card deck, what is the probability that the card is of Hearts? (The deck includes 13 of each suit clubs, diamonds, hearts, and spades)

A. $\frac{1}{3}$
B. $\frac{1}{4}$
C. $\frac{1}{6}$
D. $\frac{1}{78}$

44) Ella bought a pair of gloves for $13.59. She gave the clerk $20.00. How much change should she get back?

A. $4.51
B. $6.41
C. $7.51
D. $8.51

45) $\frac{5\times 20}{80}$ is closest estimate to?

A. 1.01
B. 1.1
C. 1.3
D. 1.4

46) If 60% of A is 30% of B, then B is what percent of A?

A. 2%
B. 20%
C. 200%
D. 300%

47) $\frac{3}{4}+\frac{\frac{-3}{5}}{\frac{6}{10}}=?$

A. $\frac{1}{4}$

B. $\frac{1}{2}$

C. $-\frac{1}{4}$

D. $-\frac{1}{2}$

IF YOU FINISH BEFORE TIME IS CALLED, YOU MAY CHECK YOUR WORK ON THIS SECTION.

STOP

ISEE Middle Level Math Practice Test 2

2019 - 2020

Two Parts

Total number of questions: 84

Part 1 (Quantitative Reasoning): 37 questions

Part 2 (Mathematics Achievement): 47 questions

Total time for two parts: 75 Minutes

ISEE Middle Level Practice Test Answer Sheets

Remove (or photocopy) this answer sheet and use it to complete the practice test.

ISEE Middle Level Practice Test 2

Quantitative Reasoning

1	Ⓐ Ⓑ Ⓒ Ⓓ	25	Ⓐ Ⓑ Ⓒ Ⓓ
2	Ⓐ Ⓑ Ⓒ Ⓓ	26	Ⓐ Ⓑ Ⓒ Ⓓ
3	Ⓐ Ⓑ Ⓒ Ⓓ	27	Ⓐ Ⓑ Ⓒ Ⓓ
4	Ⓐ Ⓑ Ⓒ Ⓓ	28	Ⓐ Ⓑ Ⓒ Ⓓ
5	Ⓐ Ⓑ Ⓒ Ⓓ	29	Ⓐ Ⓑ Ⓒ Ⓓ
6	Ⓐ Ⓑ Ⓒ Ⓓ	30	Ⓐ Ⓑ Ⓒ Ⓓ
7	Ⓐ Ⓑ Ⓒ Ⓓ	31	Ⓐ Ⓑ Ⓒ Ⓓ
8	Ⓐ Ⓑ Ⓒ Ⓓ	32	Ⓐ Ⓑ Ⓒ Ⓓ
9	Ⓐ Ⓑ Ⓒ Ⓓ	33	Ⓐ Ⓑ Ⓒ Ⓓ
10	Ⓐ Ⓑ Ⓒ Ⓓ	34	Ⓐ Ⓑ Ⓒ Ⓓ
11	Ⓐ Ⓑ Ⓒ Ⓓ	35	Ⓐ Ⓑ Ⓒ Ⓓ
12	Ⓐ Ⓑ Ⓒ Ⓓ	36	Ⓐ Ⓑ Ⓒ Ⓓ
13	Ⓐ Ⓑ Ⓒ Ⓓ	37	Ⓐ Ⓑ Ⓒ Ⓓ
14	Ⓐ Ⓑ Ⓒ Ⓓ		
15	Ⓐ Ⓑ Ⓒ Ⓓ		
16	Ⓐ Ⓑ Ⓒ Ⓓ		
17	Ⓐ Ⓑ Ⓒ Ⓓ		
18	Ⓐ Ⓑ Ⓒ Ⓓ		
19	Ⓐ Ⓑ Ⓒ Ⓓ		
20	Ⓐ Ⓑ Ⓒ Ⓓ		
21	Ⓐ Ⓑ Ⓒ Ⓓ		
22	Ⓐ Ⓑ Ⓒ Ⓓ		
23	Ⓐ Ⓑ Ⓒ Ⓓ		
24	Ⓐ Ⓑ Ⓒ Ⓓ		

Mathematics Achievement

1	Ⓐ Ⓑ Ⓒ Ⓓ	25	Ⓐ Ⓑ Ⓒ Ⓓ
2	Ⓐ Ⓑ Ⓒ Ⓓ	26	Ⓐ Ⓑ Ⓒ Ⓓ
3	Ⓐ Ⓑ Ⓒ Ⓓ	27	Ⓐ Ⓑ Ⓒ Ⓓ
4	Ⓐ Ⓑ Ⓒ Ⓓ	28	Ⓐ Ⓑ Ⓒ Ⓓ
5	Ⓐ Ⓑ Ⓒ Ⓓ	29	Ⓐ Ⓑ Ⓒ Ⓓ
6	Ⓐ Ⓑ Ⓒ Ⓓ	30	Ⓐ Ⓑ Ⓒ Ⓓ
7	Ⓐ Ⓑ Ⓒ Ⓓ	31	Ⓐ Ⓑ Ⓒ Ⓓ
8	Ⓐ Ⓑ Ⓒ Ⓓ	32	Ⓐ Ⓑ Ⓒ Ⓓ
9	Ⓐ Ⓑ Ⓒ Ⓓ	33	Ⓐ Ⓑ Ⓒ Ⓓ
10	Ⓐ Ⓑ Ⓒ Ⓓ	34	Ⓐ Ⓑ Ⓒ Ⓓ
11	Ⓐ Ⓑ Ⓒ Ⓓ	35	Ⓐ Ⓑ Ⓒ Ⓓ
12	Ⓐ Ⓑ Ⓒ Ⓓ	36	Ⓐ Ⓑ Ⓒ Ⓓ
13	Ⓐ Ⓑ Ⓒ Ⓓ	37	Ⓐ Ⓑ Ⓒ Ⓓ
14	Ⓐ Ⓑ Ⓒ Ⓓ	38	Ⓐ Ⓑ Ⓒ Ⓓ
15	Ⓐ Ⓑ Ⓒ Ⓓ	39	Ⓐ Ⓑ Ⓒ Ⓓ
16	Ⓐ Ⓑ Ⓒ Ⓓ	40	Ⓐ Ⓑ Ⓒ Ⓓ
17	Ⓐ Ⓑ Ⓒ Ⓓ	41	Ⓐ Ⓑ Ⓒ Ⓓ
18	Ⓐ Ⓑ Ⓒ Ⓓ	42	Ⓐ Ⓑ Ⓒ Ⓓ
19	Ⓐ Ⓑ Ⓒ Ⓓ	43	Ⓐ Ⓑ Ⓒ Ⓓ
20	Ⓐ Ⓑ Ⓒ Ⓓ	44	Ⓐ Ⓑ Ⓒ Ⓓ
21	Ⓐ Ⓑ Ⓒ Ⓓ	45	Ⓐ Ⓑ Ⓒ Ⓓ
22	Ⓐ Ⓑ Ⓒ Ⓓ	46	Ⓐ Ⓑ Ⓒ Ⓓ
23	Ⓐ Ⓑ Ⓒ Ⓓ	47	Ⓐ Ⓑ Ⓒ Ⓓ
24	Ⓐ Ⓑ Ⓒ Ⓓ		

ISEE Middle Level Math Practice Test 2

Section 1

37 questions

Total time for this section: 35 Minutes

You may NOT use a calculator for this test

1) What is the value of x in the following equation?

$$\frac{7^x}{7} = 343$$

A. 4
B. 5
C. 8
D. 12

2) In following shape y equals to?

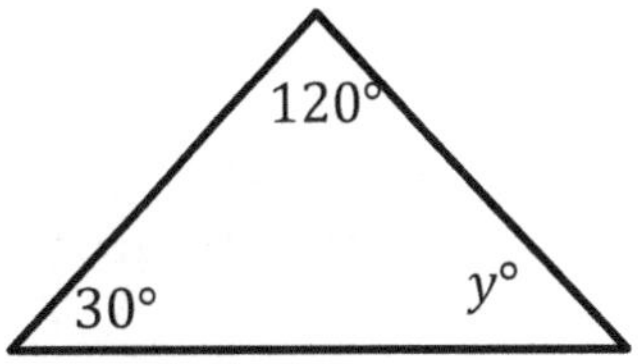

A. 120°
B. 30°
C. 25.5°
D. 20°

3) Which of the following shows the numbers in increasing order?

A. $\frac{1}{3}, \frac{8}{12}, \frac{4}{7}, \frac{3}{4}$
B. $\frac{1}{3}, \frac{4}{7}, \frac{8}{12}, \frac{3}{4}$
C. $\frac{4}{7}, \frac{3}{4}, \frac{8}{12}, \frac{1}{3}$
D. $\frac{8}{12}, \frac{3}{4}, \frac{4}{7}, \frac{1}{3}$

4) If an object travels at $0.4\ cm$ per second, how many meters does it travel in 5 hours?

A. $88.2\ m$
B. $76.4\ m$
C. $72\ m$
D. $43.2\ m$

5) If the ratio of home fans to visiting fans in a crowd is $3:2$ and all 24,000 seats in a stadium are filled, how many visiting fans are in attendance?

A. 96,000
B. 9,600
C. 960
D. 96

6) What's the approximate circumference of a circle that has a diameter of $17m$?

A. $53.38\ m$
B. $71.9\ m$
C. $97.25\ m$
D. $100\ m$

7) What is the lowest common multiple of 24 and 36?
A. 48
B. 72
C. 108
D. 864

8) What is the area of the shaded region? (one fourth of the circle is shaded) (Diameter = 8)
A. 4π
B. 6π
C. 8π
D. 9π

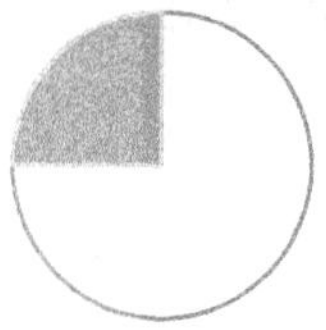

9) An item in the store originally priced at $200 was marked down 30%. What is the final sale price of the item?
A. $240
B. $204
C. $200
D. $140

10) A shirt costing $300 is discounted 15%. After a month, the shirt is discounted another 25%. Which of the following expressions can be used to find the selling price of the shirt?
A. (300) (0.70)
B. (300) – 300 (0.30)
C. (300)(0.15) – (400) (0.15)
D. (300) (0.85) (0.75)

11) If a car has 70-liter petrol and after one hour driving the car use 5-liter petrol, how much petrol remaining after x-hours?
A. $5x - 70$
B. $70 + 5x$
C. $70 - 5x$
D. $70 - x$

12) Solve for x: $4 + x + 8\left(\frac{x}{4}\right) = 2x + 12$
A. 8
B. 5.5
C. 4
D. 4.5

13) The area of the trapezoid below is 136. What is the value of x?

A. 7
B. 8
C. 10
D. 11

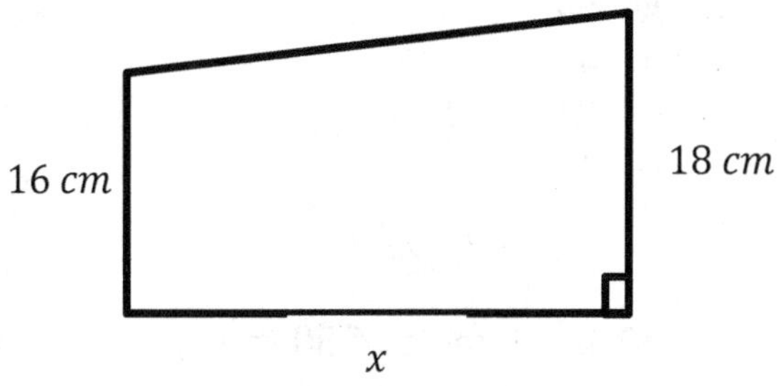

14) Find $\frac{1}{3}$ of $\frac{1}{2}$ of $\frac{3}{5}$ of 280?

A. 28
B. 30
C. 31
D. 2

15) If $x \leq a$ is the solution of $6 + 3x \leq 21$, what is the value of a?

A. $21x$
B. 5
C. -5
D. $15x$

16) 7 liters of water are poured into an aquarium that's $25cm$ long, $5cm$ wide, and $70cm$ high. How many cm will the water level in the aquarium rise due to this added water? $(1\ liter\ of\ water\ =\ 1{,}000\ cm^3)$

A. 80
B. 56
C. 49
D. 10

17) If $4f + 4g = 4x - 2y$ and $g = 2y - 6x$, what is $2f$?

A. $5x + y$
B. $14x + 3y$
C. $14x - 5y$
D. $y - 3x$

18) What is the value of $\frac{-\frac{13}{3} \times \frac{4}{5}}{\frac{10}{30}}$?

A. -10.4
B. 10.4
C. $-\frac{1}{9}$
D. $\frac{1}{9}$

19) What is the perimeter of the following parallelogram?

A. 54
B. 44
C. 24
D. 17

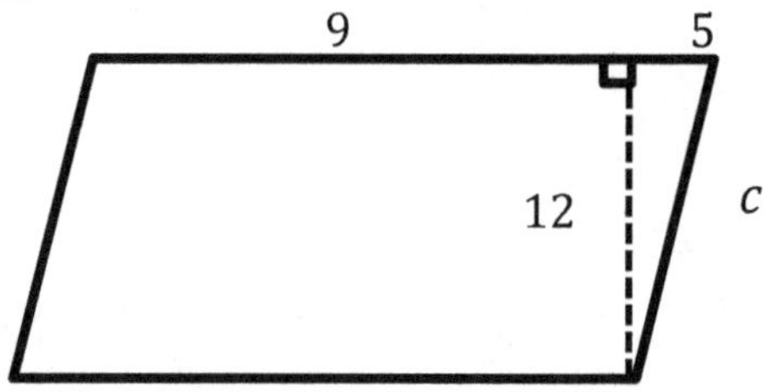

20) In a bundle of 50 fruits, 6 are apples and the rest are bananas. What percent of the bundle is composed of apples?

A. 30%
B. 25%
C. 12%
D. 10%

21) 3 less than twice a positive integer is 71. What is the integer?

A. 37
B. 40
C. 42
D. 44

22) If Joe was making \$8.50 per hour and got a raise of \$0.35 per hour, approximately what percentage increase was the raise?

A. 2%
B. 2.67%
C. 3.33%
D. 4.00%

23) Which is the equivalent temperature of $140°F$ in Celsius? ($C = Celsius$)

$$C = \frac{5}{9}(F - 32)$$

A. 32
B. 38.5
C. 50
D. 60

24) The average of $14, 16, 21$ and x is 20. What is the value of x?

A. 9
B. 15
C. 18
D. 29

25) What is the value of mode and median in the following set of numbers?

$$2, 3, 3, 6, 5, 5, 4, 4, 6, 2, 2$$

A. Mode: 2 Median: 4
B. Mode: 2, Median: 4
C. Mode: 2, 3 Median: 5
D. Mode: 3 Median: 4

Quantitative Comparisons

Direction: Questions 26 to 37 are Quantitative Comparisons Questions. Using the information provided in each question, compare the quantity in column A to the quantity in Column B. Choose on your answer sheet grid

A if the quantity in Column A is greater
B if the quantity in Column B is greater
C if the two quantities are equal
D if the relationship cannot be determined from the information given

26)

Column A	Column B
$\frac{\sqrt{64-48}}{\sqrt{25-9}}$	$\frac{(7-4)}{(8-3)}$

27) $2x^5 - 9 = 477$

$\frac{1}{3} - \frac{y}{5} = -\frac{7}{15}$

Quantity A	Quantity B
x	y

28) The sum of 3 consecutive integers is -45.

Column A	Column B
The largest of these integers	-16

29)

Column A	Column B
$4^2 - 2^4$	$2^4 - 4^2$

30) A computer costs $\$250$.

Column A	**Column B**
A sales tax at 8% of the computer cost	$\$20$

31) A

Column A	**Column B**
The slope of the line $4x + 2y = 7$	The slope of the line that passes through points $(2, 5)$ and $(3, 3)$

32)

Quantity A	Quantity B
The least prime factor of 55	The least prime factor of 210

33)

Column A	**Column B**
$\sqrt{144 - 81}$	$\sqrt{144} - \sqrt{81}$

34) 6 percent of x is equal to 5 percent of y, where x and y are positive numbers.

Quantity A	Quantity B
x	y

35)

Quantity A	Quantity B
$(-5)^4$	5^4

36)

Quantity A	Quantity B
$(1.88)^4(1.88)^8$	$(1.88)^{12}$

37) x is a positive number.

Quantity A	Quantity B
x^{10}	x^{20}

IF YOU FINISH BEFORE TIME IS CALLED, YOU MAY CHECK YOUR WORK ON THIS SECTION ONLY. DO NOT TURN TO OTHER SECTION IN THE TEST.

STOP

ISEE Middle Level Math

Practice Test 2

Section 2

47 questions

Total time for this section: 40 Minutes

You may NOT use a calculator for this test.

1) Which of the following is not synonym for 20^2?

A. 20 cubed
B. 20 squared
C. The square of 20
D. 20 to the second power

2) What is the value of x in the following equation?

$$3^x + 28 = 55$$

A. 3
B. 4
C. 5
D. 6

3) If angles A and B are angles of a parallelogram, what is the sum of the measures of the two angles?

A. 360 degrees
B. 180 degrees
C. 90 degrees
D. Cannot be determined

4) If $x =$ lowest common multiple of 10 and 35, then $\frac{x}{5} + 2$ equal to?

A. 70
B. 58
C. 46
D. 16

5) If the area of the following trapezoid is 30, what is the perimeter of the trapezoid?

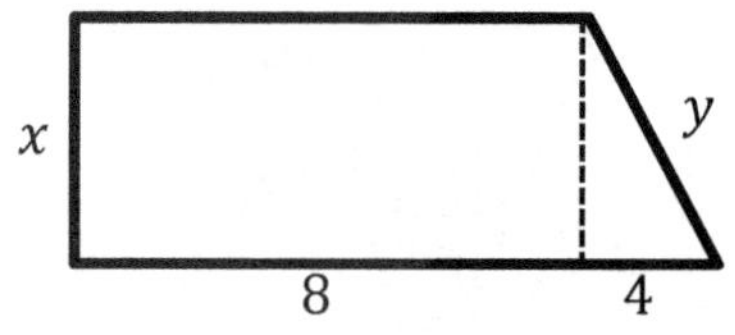

A. 25
B. 28
C. 45
D. 55

6) A swing moves from one extreme point (point A) to the opposite extreme point (point B) in 20 seconds. How long does it take that the swing moves 5 times from point A to point B and returns to point A?
A. 400 seconds
B. 200 seconds
C. 150 seconds
D. 100 seconds

7) There are 2 cars moving in the same direction on a road. A red car is 12 km ahead of a blue car. If the speed of the red car is 40 km per $hour$ and the speed of the blue car is $1\frac{2}{5}$ of the red car, how many minutes will it take the blue car to catch the red car?
A. 8.5
B. 15
C. 30
D. 45

8) In two successive years, the population of a town is increased by 10% and 25%. What percent of the population is increased after two years?
A. 25%
B. 35%
C. 36%
D. 37%

9) $5 + 8 \times (-2) - \ [4 + 22 \times 5] \div 6 \ = ?$

A. 120
B. 88
C. -30
D. -20

10) In 1989, the average worker's income increased $\$2,500$ per year starting from $\$26,000$ annual salary. Which equation represents income greater than average?
(I = income, x = number of years after 1989)

A. $\text{I} > 2{,}500x + 26{,}000$
B. $\text{I} > -2{,}500x + 26{,}000$
C. $\text{I} < -2{,}500x + 26{,}000$
D. $\text{I} < 2{,}500x - 26{,}000$

11) Which of the following angles is obtuse?

A. 10 degrees
B. 30 degrees
C. 189 degrees
D. 120 degrees

12) Mr. Jones saves $2,500 out of his monthly family income of $65,000. What fractional part of his income does he save?

A. $\frac{1}{26}$
B. $\frac{1}{11}$
C. $\frac{3}{26}$
D. $\frac{2}{15}$

13) Anita's trick–or–treat bag contains 13 pieces of chocolate, 19 suckers, 19 pieces of gum, 25 pieces of licorice. If she randomly pulls a piece of candy from her bag, what is the probability of her pulling out a piece of sucker

A. $\frac{1}{3}$
B. $\frac{1}{4}$
C. $\frac{1}{5}$
D. $\frac{1}{19}$

14) 110 is equal to?

A. $20-(4\times 10)+(6\times 30)$
B. $\left(\frac{11}{8}\times 72\right)+\left(\frac{125}{5}\right)$
C. $\left(\left(\frac{30}{4}+\frac{13}{2}\right)\times 7\right)-\frac{11}{2}+\frac{110}{4}$
D. $(2\times 10)+(50\times 1.5)+15$

15) What is the difference in area between a $8\ cm$ by $4\ cm$ rectangle and a circle with diameter of $8\ cm$? ($\pi = 3$)

A. $49\ cm$
B. $40\ cm$
C. $39\ cm$
D. $16\ cm$

16) Solve the following equation?

$$(x^2 + 2x + 1) = 64$$

A. $-9, -7$
B. $-9, 7$
C. -9
D. 7

17) What is ratio of perimeter of figure A to area of figure B?

A. $\frac{1}{3}$
B. $\frac{3}{8}$
C. 3
D. 5

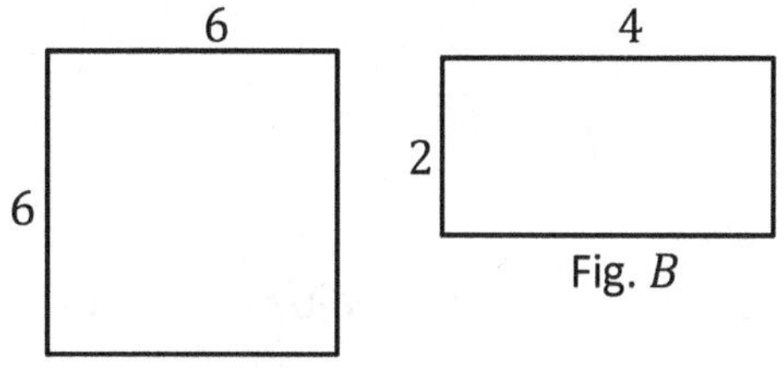

Fig. A

18) $\frac{18\times21}{5}$ is closest estimate to?

A. 75.6
B. 68.7
C. 50.6
D. 40.7

19) How many possible outfit combinations come from four shirts, two slacks, and five ties?

A. 60
B. 40
C. 16
D. 10

20) When a number is multiplied to itself and added by 9, the result is 25. What is the value of the number?

A. 4 or -4
B. 5 or -5
C. 4
D. 5

21) If you invest $\$2,000$ at an annual rate of 8%, how much interest will you earn after one year?

A. $16,000$
B. $16,00$
C. 380
D. 160

22) What is the value of x in the equation: $\frac{x}{4} + \frac{5}{4} = 5$?

A. 15
B. 10
C. 8
D. 5

23) If $y = 5ab + 3b^3$, what is y when $a = 3$ and $b = 2$?

A. 64
B. 65
C. 55
D. 54

24) What is the absolute value of the quantity six minus ten?

A. -4
B. 10
C. -10
D. 4

25) Which of the following angles can represent the three angles of an equilateral triangle?

A. $45°, 90°, 45°$
B. $50°, 50°, 80°$
C. $60°, 60°, 60°$
D. $55°, 35°, 90°$

26) In the following equation, what is the value of $x + y$?

$$9x - 10 = 5\left(\frac{4}{5}x - y\right) + 5$$

A. 15
B. -15
C. 3
D. -3

27) How many tiles of $3\ cm^2$ is needed to cover a floor of dimension $7\ cm$ by $27\ cm$?

A. 12
B. 38
C. 63
D. 66

28) Two-kilogram apple and three-kilograms orange cost $\$21$. If the price of one-kilogram of apple is twice the price of one-kilogram of orange, how much does one-kilogram apple cost?
A. $\$8$
B. $\$6$
C. $\$4$
D. $\$1$

29) Which is **NOT** a prime number?
A. 181
B. 151
C. 131
D. 122

30) Each of the x students in a team may invite up to 6 friends to a party. What is the maximum number of students and guests who might attend the party?
A. $6x + 6$
B. $6x$
C. $x + 6$
D. $7x$

31) Calculate the approximate circumference of the following circle. (the diameter is 10)

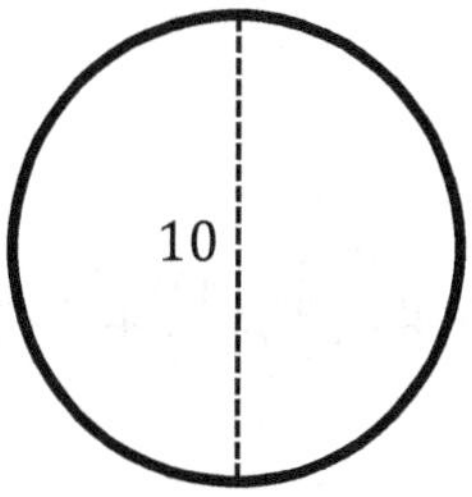

A. 1,267
B. 314
C. 31
D. 10

32) $280\ minutes$=...?
A. $5\ Hours$
B. $4.6\ Hours$
C. $3.5\ Hours$
D. $0.5\ Hours$

33) There are three boxes, a red box, a blue box, and a yellow box. If the weight of the red box is $60\ kg$ and it is 80% of the weight of the blue box, and the weight of the blue box is 120% of the weight of the yellow box, what is the weight of all boxes?
A. $197.5\ kg$
B. $210.5\ kg$
C. $280\ kg$
D. $320\ kg$

34) In the figure below, line A is parallel to line B. What is the value of angle x?

A. 35 degree
B. 40 degree
C. 100 degree
D. 140 degree

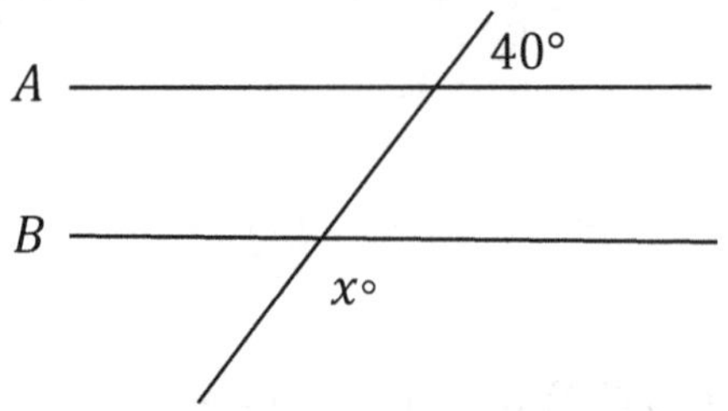

35) Jim drove 350 miles and it took him approximately 9 hours. How many miles per hour was his average speed?
A. about 34.7 miles per hour
B. about 38.8 miles per hour
C. about 48.5 miles per hour
D. about 49.5 miles per hour

36) Three people go to a restaurant. Their bill comes to $58.00. They decided to split the cost. One person pays $7.5, the next person pays 2 times that amount. How much will the third person have to pay?
A. $34.50
B. $35.50
C. $41.00
D. $45.00

37) $\left(((-15) + 40) \times \frac{1}{5}\right) + (-15)$?
A. 5
B. 10
C. -5
D. -10

38) What is 13,8210 in scientific notation?
A. 138.21×10^3
B. 13.821×10^4
C. 0.13821×10^6
D. 1.3821×10^5

39) What is the value of $(10 - 6)!$?
A. 20
B. 24
C. 26
D. 28

40) What is the perimeter of the below right triangle?

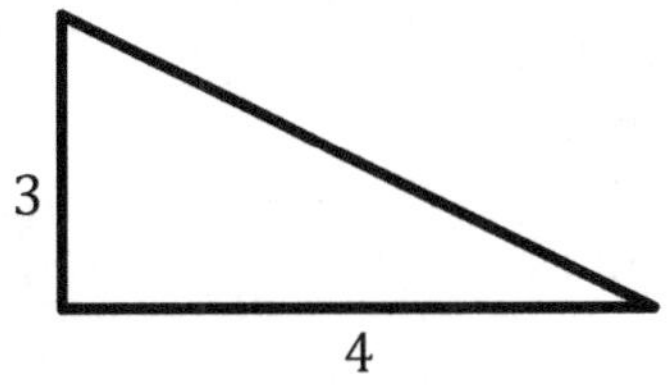

A. 20
B. 18
C. 15
D. 12

41) If 150% of a number is equal to 30% of 80, then what is the number?
A. 16
B. 15.5
C. 14.66
D. 12.25

42) In a department of a company, the ratio of employees with Bachelor's Degree to employees with high school Diploma is 1 to 4. If there are 24 employees with Bachelor's Degree in this department, how many employees with High School Diploma should be moved to other departments to change the ratio of the number of employees with Bachelor's Degree to the number of employees with High School Diploma to 3 to 4 in this department?
A. 64
B. 54
C. 10
D. 12

43) What is x in the following right triangle?

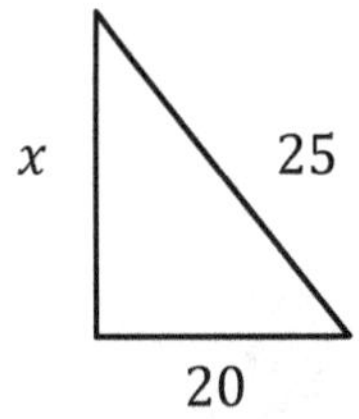

A. $\sqrt{399}$
B. 15
C. 20
D. $\sqrt{402}$

44) The average weight of 20 girls in a class is $65\ kg$ and the average weight of 35 boys in the same class is $72\ kg$. What is the average weight of all the 55 students in that class?
A. 61.28
B. 61.68
C. 62.90
D. 69.45

45) An angle is equal to one ninth of its supplement. What is the measure of that angle?
A. 18
B. 30
C. 45
D. 60

46) What is the difference of smallest 5–digit number and biggest 5–digit number?

A. 66,666
B. 67,899
C. 88,888
D. 89,999

47) John traveled $140\ km$ in 5 hours and Alice traveled $210\ km$ in 3 hours. What is the ratio of the average speed of John to average speed of Alice?

A. $2:5$
B. $5:2$
C. $5:9$
D. $5:6$

IF YOU FINISH BEFORE TIME IS CALLED, YOU MAY CHECK YOUR WORK ON THIS SECTION.

STOP

ISEE Middle Level Math Practice Test 3

2019 - 2020

Two Parts

Total number of questions: 84

Part 1 (Quantitative Reasoning): 37 questions

Part 2 (Mathematics Achievement): 47 questions

Total time for two parts: 75 Minutes

ISEE Middle Level Practice Test Answer Sheets

Remove (or photocopy) this answer sheet and use it to complete the practice test.

ISEE Middle Level Practice Test 3

Quantitative Reasoning				Mathematics Achievement			
1	Ⓐ Ⓑ Ⓒ Ⓓ	25	Ⓐ Ⓑ Ⓒ Ⓓ	1	Ⓐ Ⓑ Ⓒ Ⓓ	25	Ⓐ Ⓑ Ⓒ Ⓓ
2	Ⓐ Ⓑ Ⓒ Ⓓ	26	Ⓐ Ⓑ Ⓒ Ⓓ	2	Ⓐ Ⓑ Ⓒ Ⓓ	26	Ⓐ Ⓑ Ⓒ Ⓓ
3	Ⓐ Ⓑ Ⓒ Ⓓ	27	Ⓐ Ⓑ Ⓒ Ⓓ	3	Ⓐ Ⓑ Ⓒ Ⓓ	27	Ⓐ Ⓑ Ⓒ Ⓓ
4	Ⓐ Ⓑ Ⓒ Ⓓ	28	Ⓐ Ⓑ Ⓒ Ⓓ	4	Ⓐ Ⓑ Ⓒ Ⓓ	28	Ⓐ Ⓑ Ⓒ Ⓓ
5	Ⓐ Ⓑ Ⓒ Ⓓ	29	Ⓐ Ⓑ Ⓒ Ⓓ	5	Ⓐ Ⓑ Ⓒ Ⓓ	29	Ⓐ Ⓑ Ⓒ Ⓓ
6	Ⓐ Ⓑ Ⓒ Ⓓ	30	Ⓐ Ⓑ Ⓒ Ⓓ	6	Ⓐ Ⓑ Ⓒ Ⓓ	30	Ⓐ Ⓑ Ⓒ Ⓓ
7	Ⓐ Ⓑ Ⓒ Ⓓ	31	Ⓐ Ⓑ Ⓒ Ⓓ	7	Ⓐ Ⓑ Ⓒ Ⓓ	31	Ⓐ Ⓑ Ⓒ Ⓓ
8	Ⓐ Ⓑ Ⓒ Ⓓ	32	Ⓐ Ⓑ Ⓒ Ⓓ	8	Ⓐ Ⓑ Ⓒ Ⓓ	32	Ⓐ Ⓑ Ⓒ Ⓓ
9	Ⓐ Ⓑ Ⓒ Ⓓ	33	Ⓐ Ⓑ Ⓒ Ⓓ	9	Ⓐ Ⓑ Ⓒ Ⓓ	33	Ⓐ Ⓑ Ⓒ Ⓓ
10	Ⓐ Ⓑ Ⓒ Ⓓ	34	Ⓐ Ⓑ Ⓒ Ⓓ	10	Ⓐ Ⓑ Ⓒ Ⓓ	34	Ⓐ Ⓑ Ⓒ Ⓓ
11	Ⓐ Ⓑ Ⓒ Ⓓ	35	Ⓐ Ⓑ Ⓒ Ⓓ	11	Ⓐ Ⓑ Ⓒ Ⓓ	35	Ⓐ Ⓑ Ⓒ Ⓓ
12	Ⓐ Ⓑ Ⓒ Ⓓ	36	Ⓐ Ⓑ Ⓒ Ⓓ	12	Ⓐ Ⓑ Ⓒ Ⓓ	36	Ⓐ Ⓑ Ⓒ Ⓓ
13	Ⓐ Ⓑ Ⓒ Ⓓ	37	Ⓐ Ⓑ Ⓒ Ⓓ	13	Ⓐ Ⓑ Ⓒ Ⓓ	37	Ⓐ Ⓑ Ⓒ Ⓓ
14	Ⓐ Ⓑ Ⓒ Ⓓ			14	Ⓐ Ⓑ Ⓒ Ⓓ	38	Ⓐ Ⓑ Ⓒ Ⓓ
15	Ⓐ Ⓑ Ⓒ Ⓓ			15	Ⓐ Ⓑ Ⓒ Ⓓ	39	Ⓐ Ⓑ Ⓒ Ⓓ
16	Ⓐ Ⓑ Ⓒ Ⓓ			16	Ⓐ Ⓑ Ⓒ Ⓓ	40	Ⓐ Ⓑ Ⓒ Ⓓ
17	Ⓐ Ⓑ Ⓒ Ⓓ			17	Ⓐ Ⓑ Ⓒ Ⓓ	41	Ⓐ Ⓑ Ⓒ Ⓓ
18	Ⓐ Ⓑ Ⓒ Ⓓ			18	Ⓐ Ⓑ Ⓒ Ⓓ	42	Ⓐ Ⓑ Ⓒ Ⓓ
19	Ⓐ Ⓑ Ⓒ Ⓓ			19	Ⓐ Ⓑ Ⓒ Ⓓ	43	Ⓐ Ⓑ Ⓒ Ⓓ
20	Ⓐ Ⓑ Ⓒ Ⓓ			20	Ⓐ Ⓑ Ⓒ Ⓓ	44	Ⓐ Ⓑ Ⓒ Ⓓ
21	Ⓐ Ⓑ Ⓒ Ⓓ			21	Ⓐ Ⓑ Ⓒ Ⓓ	45	Ⓐ Ⓑ Ⓒ Ⓓ
22	Ⓐ Ⓑ Ⓒ Ⓓ			22	Ⓐ Ⓑ Ⓒ Ⓓ	46	Ⓐ Ⓑ Ⓒ Ⓓ
23	Ⓐ Ⓑ Ⓒ Ⓓ			23	Ⓐ Ⓑ Ⓒ Ⓓ	47	Ⓐ Ⓑ Ⓒ Ⓓ
24	Ⓐ Ⓑ Ⓒ Ⓓ			24	Ⓐ Ⓑ Ⓒ Ⓓ		

ISEE Middle Level Math

Practice Test 3

Section 1

37 questions

Total time for this section: 35 Minutes

You may NOT use a calculator for this test.

1) Which of the following shows the numbers in descending order?

A. $\frac{1}{5}, \frac{2}{5}, \frac{3}{8}, \frac{5}{4}$

B. $\frac{1}{5}, \frac{2}{5}, \frac{5}{4}, \frac{3}{8}$

C. $\frac{1}{5}, \frac{3}{8}, \frac{2}{5}, \frac{5}{4}$

D. $\frac{1}{5}, \frac{5}{4}, \frac{3}{8}, \frac{2}{5}$

2) $542{,}357{,}841 \times 0.0001$?

A. $542{,}357.841$

B. $54{,}235.7841$

C. $5{,}423.57841$

D. 542.357841

3) Jim purchased a table for 16% off and saved $\$40$. What was the original price of the table?

A. $\$90$

B. $\$110$

C. $\$250$

D. 260

4) A $\$42$ shirt now selling for $\$27$ is discounted by what percent?

A. 25%

B. 35%

C. 40%

D. 60%

5) If $f = 2x - 3y$ and $g = x + 7y$, what is $4f + g$?

A. $3x + y$

B. $3x - 2y$

C. $9x - 5y$

D. $9x - 3y$

6) Solve. $\frac{-48 \times 0.5}{6}$

A. -16

B. -4

C. 4

D. 16

7) What is the value of x in the following equation? $8^x = 512$

A. 6
B. 4
C. 3
D. 2

8) The score of Emma was half as that of Ava and the score of Mia was twice that of Ava. If the score of Mia was 80, what is the score of Emma?

A. 20
B. 28
C. 30
D. 40

9) The area of a circle is $81\ \pi$. What is the circumference of the circle?

A. $8\ \pi$
B. $18\ \pi$
C. $32\ \pi$
D. $81\ \pi$

10) Round off the result of 1.16×7.4 to the nearest tenth?

A. 7.2
B. 7.5
C. 8.2
D. 8.6

11) What is the value of x in the following figure?

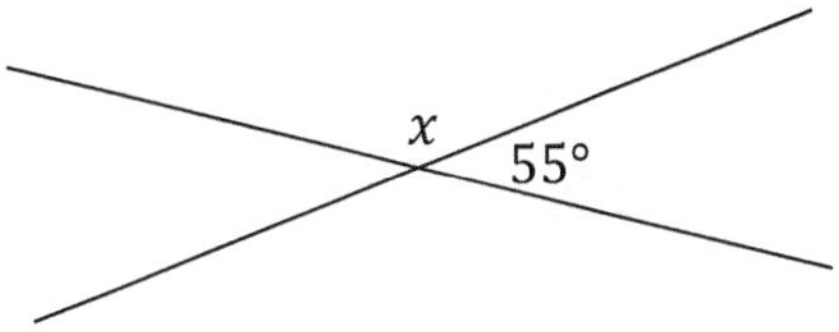

A. 25°
B. 55°
C. 115°
D. 125°

12) Two third of 9 is equal to $\frac{2}{7}$ of what number?

A. 50
B. 30
C. 25
D. 21

13) Which number is closest to the square root of 170?

A. 50
B. 20
C. 13
D. 9

14) A box has a height of 12 cm, a length of 8 cm and volume of 960 cm^3. What is its width?
A. 24 cm
B. 16 cm
C. 12 cm
D. 10 cm

15) The perimeter of the trapezoid below is 58. What is its area?

A. 252 cm^2
B. 239 cm^2
C. 235 cm^2
D. 231 cm^2

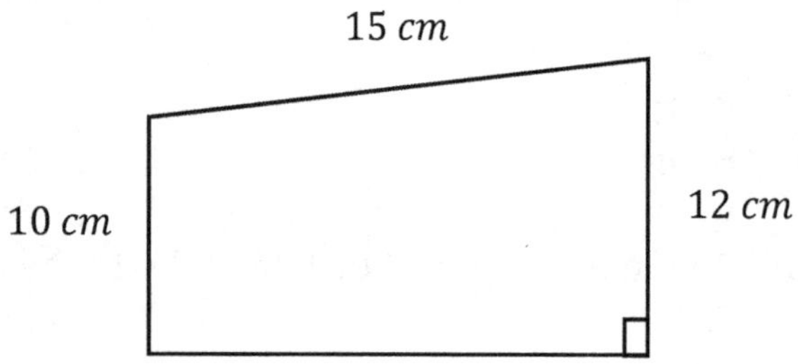

16) The price of a laptop is decreased by 60% to \$460. What is its original price?
A. \$320
B. \$460
C. \$890
D. \$1,150

17) Find $\frac{1}{5}$ of $\frac{1}{3}$ of 120?
A. 4
B. 8
C. 12
D. 20

18) The ratio of boys to girls in a class is 3: 8. If there are 55 students in the class, how many more boys should be enrolled to make the ratio 1: 1?
A. 4
B. 19
C. 25
D. 36

19) What is the value of x in the following equation?

$$4(x+1) = 6(x+4) - 28$$

A. 0
B. 4
C. 5.2
D. 5.5

20) A company pays its employee $\$8{,}000$ plus 4% of all sales profit. If x is all sold profit, which of the following represents the employee's revenue?

A. $0.04x$
B. $0.96x - 8{,}000$
C. $0.04x + 8{,}000$
D. $0.96x + 8{,}000$

21) Which of the following is a correct statement?

A. $\frac{3}{4} > 0.9$
B. $11\% = \frac{2}{5}$
C. $3.5 < \frac{7}{3}$
D. $\frac{6}{7} > 0.8$

22) What is the value of x in the following figure?

A. 180
B. 150
C. 125
D. 115

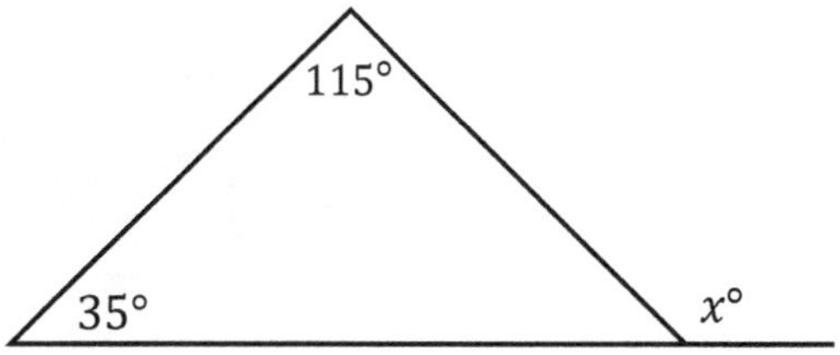

23) What is the area of a square whose diagonal is 4?

A. 4
B. 8
C. 16
D. 64

24) What is value of $-28 - (-75)$?

A. 47
B. -90
C. -47
D. 90

25) Car A use 6-liter petrol per 100 kilometers; car B use 4-liter petrol per 100 kilometers. If both cars drive 150 kilometers, how much more petrol does car A use?

A. 3
B. 9
C. 18
D. 25

Quantitative Comparisons

Direction: Questions 26 to 37 are Quantitative Comparisons Questions. Using the information provided in each question, compare the quantity in column A to the quantity in Column B. Choose on your answer sheet grid

A if the quantity in Column A is greater
B if the quantity in Column B is greater
C if the two quantities are equal
D if the relationship cannot be determined from the information given

26)

Column A	Column B
$\sqrt{25}+\sqrt{25}$	$\sqrt{100}$

27) The average age of Joe, Michelle, and Nicole is 30

Column A	Column B
The average age of Joe and Michelle	The average age of Michelle and Nicole

28)

Column A	Column B
$5+5\times 7-4$	$4+6\times 6-6$

29) $y=3x+18$

Column A	Column B
The value of x when $y=9$	-4

30)

Column A	Column B
$\sqrt{144-121}$	$\sqrt{144}-\sqrt{121}$

31) A right cylinder with radius 5 inches has volume 80π cubic inches.

Quantity A	Quantity B
The height of the cylinder	3 inches

32) x is an integer greater than zero.

Quantity A	Quantity B
$\frac{2}{x}+x$	5

33)

$$\frac{2}{5}<x<\frac{5}{9}$$

Quantity A	Quantity B
x	$\frac{5}{8}$

34) x is a positive integer.

Quantity A	Quantity B
$\frac{x^3}{3}$	$(\frac{x}{3})^3$

35) The average of 5, 6 and x is 6.

Quantity A	Quantity B
x	average of $x, x+3, x+1, -x$

36) a and b are real numbers.

$$a > b$$

Quantity A	Quantity B
$\lvert a - b \rvert$	$\lvert b - a \rvert$

37) $4x^3 - 80 = 176$
$3 - 4y = -13$

Quantity A	Quantity B
x	y

IF YOU FINISH BEFORE TIME IS CALLED, YOU MAY CHECK YOUR WORK ON THIS SECTION ONLY. DO NOT TURN TO OTHER SECTION IN THE TEST.

STOP

ISEE Middle Level Math

Practice Test 3

Section 2

47 questions

Total time for this section: 40 Minutes

You may NOT use a calculator for this test.

1) What number is 28 more than 15% of 120?
A. 50
B. 46
C. 25
D. 15

2) If a box contains red and blue balls in ratio of $2:5$, how many red balls are there if 60 blue balls are in the box?
A. 20
B. 24
C. 30
D. 35

3) $3\left(\frac{1}{2}-\frac{1}{8}\right)+6$?
A. 8
B. 7.125
C. 6.5
D. 6.375

4) In a bundle of 92 pencils, 45 are red and the rest are blue. About what percent of the bundle is composed of blue pencils?
A. 65%
B. 60%
C. 56%
D. 51%

5) What is the value of x in the following equation?

$$(x+9)^3=125$$

A. 4
B. -4
C. 2
D. -2

6) What number is 6 less than 40% of 36?
A. 4.5
B. 8.4
C. 10.2
D. 15

7) What is the difference in perimeter between a $8\ cm$ by $4\ cm$ rectangle and a circle with diameter of $18\ cm$? $(\pi = 3)$

A. $30\ cm$
B. $25\ cm$
C. $20\ cm$
D. $12\ cm$

8) Sophia purchased a sofa for $\$504$. The sofa is regularly priced at $\$600$. What was the percent discount Sophia received on the sofa?

A. 10%
B. 16%
C. 25%
D. 84%

9) When a number is subtracted from 32 and the difference is divided by that number, the result is 3. What is the value of the number?

A. 2
B. 4
C. 8
D. 12

10) 92 is equal to?

A. $2 + (3 \times 10) + (2 \times 30)$
B. $\left(\frac{10}{3} \times 27\right) + \left(\frac{5}{2} \times 2\right)$
C. $\left(\left(\frac{3}{2} + 3\right) \times \frac{18}{3}\right) + 63$
D. $(2 \times 15) + (50 \times 2) - 46$

11) If $\frac{2x}{3} = 30$, then $\frac{2x}{4} = ?$

A. 22.5
B. 20
C. 15
D. 10

12) Which of the following is the greatest number?

A. $\frac{1}{2}$
B. $\frac{7}{9}$
C. 0.80
D. 55%

13) Calculate the approximate area of the following circle. (diameter is 30 cm)

A. $1{,}257\ cm^2$
B. $706.5\ cm^2$
C. $225\ cm^2$
D. $63\ cm^2$

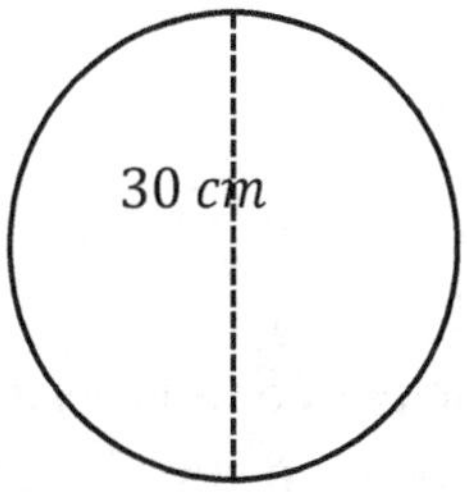

14) If 140% of a number is 98, then what is 80% of that number?
A. 56
B. 60
C. 70
D. 85

15) What is the missing term in the given numbers?

$$2, 3, 5, 8, 12, 17, \_\_, 30$$

A. 23
B. 26
C. 27
D. 30

16) Which of the following angles can represent the three angles of a triangle?
A. $50°, 50°, 90°$
B. $50°, 40°, 100°$
C. $80°, 70°, 60°$
D. $45°, 55°, 80°$

17) If paper clips cost 48 cents a dozen, how many paper clips cost two dollars?
A. 175
B. 100
C. 50
D. 25

18) When a gas tank can hold 35 gallons, how many gallons does it contain when it is $\frac{2}{7}$ full?
A. 30
B. 25
C. 15
D. 10

19) If $A \times A$ is odd, then A CANNOT be:
A. Zero
B. Prime
C. Negative
D. Odd

20) The capacity of a red box is 20% greater than a blue box. If the capacity of the red box is 36 books, how many books can be put in the blue box?
A. 9
B. 15
C. 30
D. 36

21) From last year, the price of gasoline has increased from $\$1.25$ per gallon to $\$1.85$ per gallon. The new price is what percent of the original price?
A. 72%
B. 120%
C. 148%
D. 185%

22) $198\ minutes\ = ...?$
A. $3.3\ Hours$
B. $3.16\ Hours$
C. $2\ Hours$
D. $0.3\ Hours$

23) If a gas tank can hold 45 gallons, how many gallons does it contain when it is $\frac{2}{5}$ full?
A. 60
B. 55
C. 45
D. 18

24) Which of the following is **NOT** a prime number?
A. 103
B. 101
C. 97
D. 69

25) What is the perimeter of a square that has an area of 49 square inches?
A. $144\ inches$
B. $49\ inches$
C. $28\ inches$
D. $16\ inches$

26) Jason left a $\$14.00$ tip on a lunch that cost $\$32.00$, approximately what percentage was the tip?
A. 2.5%
B. 12%
C. 32%
D. 43%

27) Two-kilograms apple and three-kilograms orange cost $\$29.4$. If one-kilogram apple costs $\$4.2$ how much does one-kilogram orange cost?
A. $\$9$
B. $\$7$
C. $\$6.5$
D. $\$5$

28) $\left(\left((-14) + 24\right) \times 2\right) + (-10)$?
A. 10
B. 5
C. 4
D. 3

29) The width of a rectangle is $5x$ and its length is $7x$. The perimeter of the rectangle is 60. What is the value of x?
A. 2.5
B. 5
C. 6
D. 10

30) Jason is 6 miles ahead of Joe running at 6.5 miles per hour and Joe is running at the speed of 8 miles per hour. How long does it take Joe to catch Jason?
A. $2\ hours$
B. $3\ hours$
C. $4\ hours$
D. $6\ hours$

31) $[7 \times (-25) + 9] - (-2) + [4 \times 4] \div 2 = ?$
A. 148
B. 132
C. -144
D. -156

32) If 35% of a class are girls, and 24% of girls play tennis, what percent of the class play tennis?
A. 8%
B. 15%
C. 20%
D. 35%

33) In a class, there are twice as many girls as boys. If the total number of students in the class is 57, how many girls are in the class?
A. 19
B. 25
C. 32
D. 36

34) At a Zoo, the ratio of lions to tigers is 5 to 1. Which of the following could NOT be the total number of lions and tigers in the zoo?
A. 36
B. 54
C. 79
D. 108

35) The price of a sofa is decreased by 20% to $\$560$. What was its original price?
A. $\$480$
B. $\$520$
C. $\$700$
D. $\$750$

36) A shaft rotates 100 times in 3.5 seconds. How many times does it rotate in 14 seconds?
A. 400
B. 250
C. 200
D. 100

37) Solve the equation for x: $10x - 16.5 = -46.5$?

A. -3
B. -2
C. 2
D. 3

38) A swimming pool holds $3{,}000$ cubic feet of water. The swimming pool is 50 feet long and 6 feet wide. How deep is the swimming pool?

A. $2\ feet$
B. $4\ feet$
C. $8\ feet$
D. $10\ feet$

39) What is the value of x in the following equation?

$$6^x = 216$$

A. 2
B. 3
C. 5
D. 6

40) What is the area of the trapezoid?

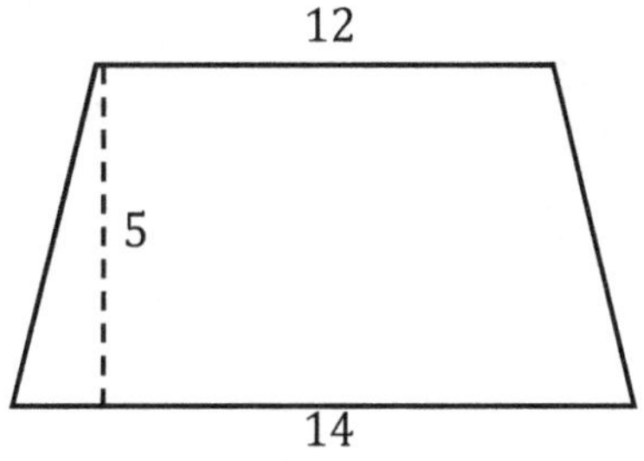

A. 25
B. 65
C. 100
D. 150

41) $14.124 \div 0.005$?

A. 2.824
B. 28.24
C. 282.24
D. $2{,}824.8$

42) What is the value of x in the following equation?

$$10 + 6(x + 2 - 2x) = 28$$

A. -1
B. 1.5
C. -2
D. 3

43) Ella bought a pair of gloves for $\$11.49$. She gave the clerk $\$20.00$. How much change should she get back?

A. $\$9.51$
B. $\$8.51$
C. $\$6.51$
D. $\$5.51$

44) If 90% of A is 30% of B, then B is what percent of A?

A. 3%
B. 30%
C. 200%
D. 300%

45) A card is drawn at random from a standard 52–card deck, what is the probability that the card is of Diamonds? (The deck includes 13 of each suit clubs, diamonds, hearts, and spades)

A. $\frac{1}{4}$
B. $\frac{1}{5}$
C. $\frac{1}{6}$
D. $\frac{1}{52}$

46) $\frac{3}{5} + \frac{\frac{-2}{5}}{\frac{4}{10}} = ?$

A. $\frac{2}{5}$
B. $\frac{1}{4}$
C. $-\frac{2}{5}$
D. $-\frac{1}{4}$

47) $\frac{7 \times 15}{60}$ is closest estimate to?

A. 1.9
B. 1.8
C. 1.6
D. 1.5

IF YOU FINISH BEFORE TIME IS CALLED, YOU MAY CHECK YOUR WORK ON THIS SECTION.

STOP

ISEE Middle Level Math Practice Test 4

2019 - 2020

Two Parts

Total number of questions: 84

Part 1 (Quantitative Reasoning): 37 questions

Part 2 (Mathematics Achievement): 47 questions

Total time for two parts: 75 Minutes

ISEE Middle Level Practice Test Answer Sheets

Remove (or photocopy) this answer sheet and use it to complete the practice test.

ISEE Middle Level Practice Test 4

Quantitative Reasoning				Mathematics Achievement			
1	Ⓐ Ⓑ Ⓒ Ⓓ	25	Ⓐ Ⓑ Ⓒ Ⓓ	1	Ⓐ Ⓑ Ⓒ Ⓓ	25	Ⓐ Ⓑ Ⓒ Ⓓ
2	Ⓐ Ⓑ Ⓒ Ⓓ	26	Ⓐ Ⓑ Ⓒ Ⓓ	2	Ⓐ Ⓑ Ⓒ Ⓓ	26	Ⓐ Ⓑ Ⓒ Ⓓ
3	Ⓐ Ⓑ Ⓒ Ⓓ	27	Ⓐ Ⓑ Ⓒ Ⓓ	3	Ⓐ Ⓑ Ⓒ Ⓓ	27	Ⓐ Ⓑ Ⓒ Ⓓ
4	Ⓐ Ⓑ Ⓒ Ⓓ	28	Ⓐ Ⓑ Ⓒ Ⓓ	4	Ⓐ Ⓑ Ⓒ Ⓓ	28	Ⓐ Ⓑ Ⓒ Ⓓ
5	Ⓐ Ⓑ Ⓒ Ⓓ	29	Ⓐ Ⓑ Ⓒ Ⓓ	5	Ⓐ Ⓑ Ⓒ Ⓓ	29	Ⓐ Ⓑ Ⓒ Ⓓ
6	Ⓐ Ⓑ Ⓒ Ⓓ	30	Ⓐ Ⓑ Ⓒ Ⓓ	6	Ⓐ Ⓑ Ⓒ Ⓓ	30	Ⓐ Ⓑ Ⓒ Ⓓ
7	Ⓐ Ⓑ Ⓒ Ⓓ	31	Ⓐ Ⓑ Ⓒ Ⓓ	7	Ⓐ Ⓑ Ⓒ Ⓓ	31	Ⓐ Ⓑ Ⓒ Ⓓ
8	Ⓐ Ⓑ Ⓒ Ⓓ	32	Ⓐ Ⓑ Ⓒ Ⓓ	8	Ⓐ Ⓑ Ⓒ Ⓓ	32	Ⓐ Ⓑ Ⓒ Ⓓ
9	Ⓐ Ⓑ Ⓒ Ⓓ	33	Ⓐ Ⓑ Ⓒ Ⓓ	9	Ⓐ Ⓑ Ⓒ Ⓓ	33	Ⓐ Ⓑ Ⓒ Ⓓ
10	Ⓐ Ⓑ Ⓒ Ⓓ	34	Ⓐ Ⓑ Ⓒ Ⓓ	10	Ⓐ Ⓑ Ⓒ Ⓓ	34	Ⓐ Ⓑ Ⓒ Ⓓ
11	Ⓐ Ⓑ Ⓒ Ⓓ	35	Ⓐ Ⓑ Ⓒ Ⓓ	11	Ⓐ Ⓑ Ⓒ Ⓓ	35	Ⓐ Ⓑ Ⓒ Ⓓ
12	Ⓐ Ⓑ Ⓒ Ⓓ	36	Ⓐ Ⓑ Ⓒ Ⓓ	12	Ⓐ Ⓑ Ⓒ Ⓓ	36	Ⓐ Ⓑ Ⓒ Ⓓ
13	Ⓐ Ⓑ Ⓒ Ⓓ	37	Ⓐ Ⓑ Ⓒ Ⓓ	13	Ⓐ Ⓑ Ⓒ Ⓓ	37	Ⓐ Ⓑ Ⓒ Ⓓ
14	Ⓐ Ⓑ Ⓒ Ⓓ			14	Ⓐ Ⓑ Ⓒ Ⓓ	38	Ⓐ Ⓑ Ⓒ Ⓓ
15	Ⓐ Ⓑ Ⓒ Ⓓ			15	Ⓐ Ⓑ Ⓒ Ⓓ	39	Ⓐ Ⓑ Ⓒ Ⓓ
16	Ⓐ Ⓑ Ⓒ Ⓓ			16	Ⓐ Ⓑ Ⓒ Ⓓ	40	Ⓐ Ⓑ Ⓒ Ⓓ
17	Ⓐ Ⓑ Ⓒ Ⓓ			17	Ⓐ Ⓑ Ⓒ Ⓓ	41	Ⓐ Ⓑ Ⓒ Ⓓ
18	Ⓐ Ⓑ Ⓒ Ⓓ			18	Ⓐ Ⓑ Ⓒ Ⓓ	42	Ⓐ Ⓑ Ⓒ Ⓓ
19	Ⓐ Ⓑ Ⓒ Ⓓ			19	Ⓐ Ⓑ Ⓒ Ⓓ	43	Ⓐ Ⓑ Ⓒ Ⓓ
20	Ⓐ Ⓑ Ⓒ Ⓓ			20	Ⓐ Ⓑ Ⓒ Ⓓ	44	Ⓐ Ⓑ Ⓒ Ⓓ
21	Ⓐ Ⓑ Ⓒ Ⓓ			21	Ⓐ Ⓑ Ⓒ Ⓓ	45	Ⓐ Ⓑ Ⓒ Ⓓ
22	Ⓐ Ⓑ Ⓒ Ⓓ			22	Ⓐ Ⓑ Ⓒ Ⓓ	46	Ⓐ Ⓑ Ⓒ Ⓓ
23	Ⓐ Ⓑ Ⓒ Ⓓ			23	Ⓐ Ⓑ Ⓒ Ⓓ	47	Ⓐ Ⓑ Ⓒ Ⓓ
24	Ⓐ Ⓑ Ⓒ Ⓓ			24	Ⓐ Ⓑ Ⓒ Ⓓ		

ISEE Middle Level Math

Practice Test 4

Section 1

37 questions

Total time for this section: 35 Minutes

You may NOT use a calculator for this test.

1) If the ratio of home fans to visiting fans in a crowd is $3:2$ and all $25,000$ seats in a stadium are filled, how many visiting fans are in attendance?
A. $100,000$
B. $10,000$
C. $1,000$
D. 100

2) In following shape y equals to?

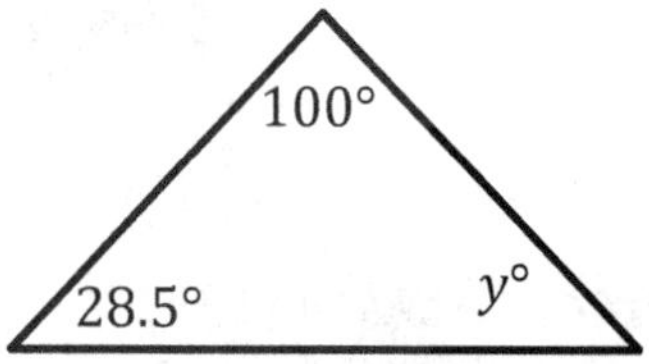

A. $128.5°$
B. $51.5°$
C. $48.5°$
D. $35°$

3) Which of the following shows the numbers in increasing order?
A. $\frac{2}{3}, \frac{8}{11}, \frac{5}{7}, \frac{3}{4}$
B. $\frac{2}{3}, \frac{5}{7}, \frac{8}{11}, \frac{3}{4}$
C. $\frac{5}{7}, \frac{3}{4}, \frac{8}{11}, \frac{2}{3}$
D. $\frac{8}{11}, \frac{3}{4}, \frac{5}{7}, \frac{2}{3}$

4) If an object travels at $0.3\ cm$ per second, how many meters does it travel in 4 hours?
A. $88.2\ m$
B. $66.4\ m$
C. $50\ m$
D. $43.2\ m$

5) What is the value of x in the following equation?

$$\frac{3^x}{9} = 243$$

A. 7
B. 5
C. 3
D. 2

6) Ava uses a 40% off coupon when buying a sweater that costs $\$40$. If she also pays 5% sales tax on the purchase, how much does she pay?
A. $\$26.95$
B. $\$25.20$
C. $\$21.7$
D. $\$14.83$

7) An item in the store originally priced at $\$300$ was marked down 20%. What is the final sale price of the item?

A. $\$240$
B. $\$204$
C. $\$200$
D. $\$195$

8) What's the circumference of a circle that has a diameter of $15\ m$? ($\pi = 3.14$)

A. $47.1\ m$
B. $94.29\ m$
C. $150\ m$
D. $225\ m$

9) What is the area of the shaded region? (one forth of the circle is shaded)
Diameter $= 12$

A. $6\ \pi$
B. $7\ \pi$
C. $8\ \pi$
D. $9\ \pi$

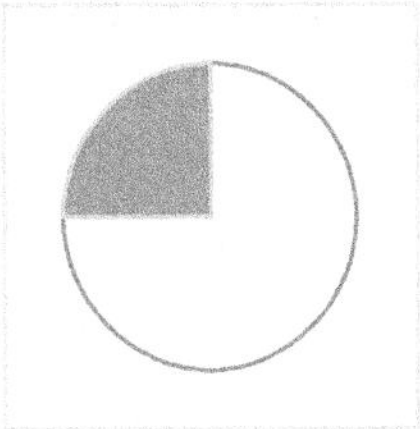

10) If a car has 80-liter petrol and after one hour driving the car use 6-liter petrol, how much petrol remaining after x-hours?

A. $6x - 80$
B. $80 + 6x$
C. $80 - 6x$
D. $80 - x$

11) A shirt costing $\$200$ is discounted 15%. After a month, the shirt is discounted another 15%. Which of the following expressions can be used to find the selling price of the shirt

A. $(200)\ (0.70)$
B. $(200) - 200\ (0.30)$
C. $(200)(0.15) - (200)\ (0.15)$
D. $(200)\ (0.85)\ (0.85)$

12) Find $\frac{1}{3}$ of $\frac{2}{5}$ of $\frac{3}{4}$ of 300?

A. 30
B. 32
C. 35
D. 45

13) If $x \le a$ is the solution of $7 + 2x \le 15$, what is the value of a?
A. $14x$
B. 4
C. -4
D. $15x$

14) The area of the trapezoid below is 132. What is the value of x?

A. 8
B. 9
C. 10
D. 11

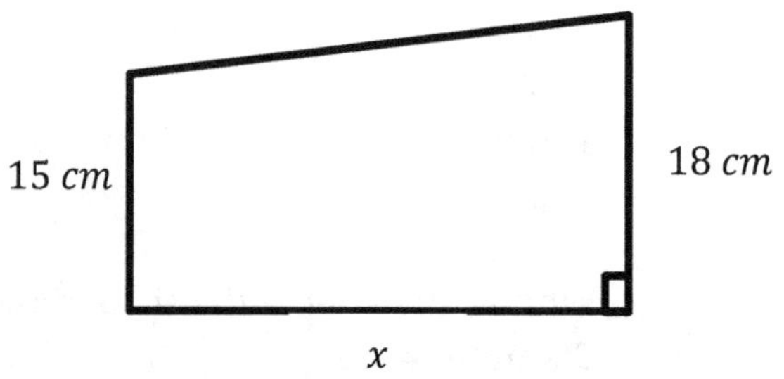

15) Solve for x: $3 + x + 6\left(\frac{x}{2}\right) = 2x + 10$
A. $\frac{13}{6}$
B. $\frac{7}{6}$
C. $\frac{7}{2}$
D. $\frac{13}{2}$

16) 6 liters of water are poured into an aquarium that's $15cm$ long, $5cm$ wide, and $90cm$ high. How many cm will the water level in the aquarium rise due to this added water? $(1\ liter\ of\ water = 1{,}000\ cm^3)$
A. 80
B. 40
C. 20
D. 10

17) If $3f + 2g = 3x + y$ and $g = 2y - 3x$, what is f?
A. $3x + y$
B. $x + 3y$
C. $3x - y$
D. $y - 3x$

18) What is the perimeter of the following parallelogram?
A. 48
B. 34
C. 24
D. 17

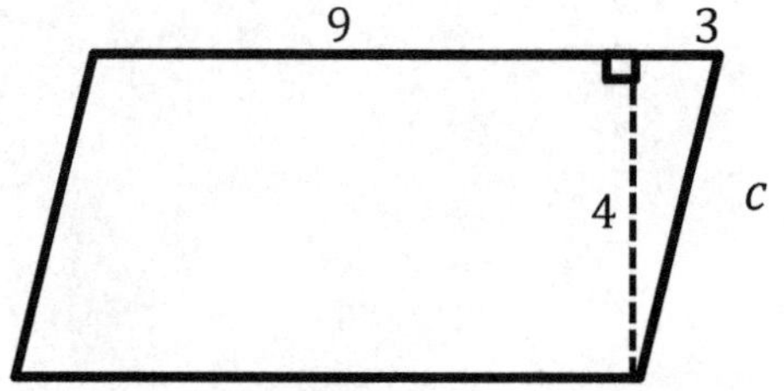

19) In a bundle of 40 fruits, 8 are apples and the rest are bananas. What percent of the bundle is composed of apples?

A. 40%
B. 25%
C. 20%
D. 15%

20) What is the value of $\frac{-\frac{11}{2}\times\frac{3}{5}}{\frac{11}{30}}$?

A. -9
B. 9
C. $-\frac{1}{9}$
D. $\frac{1}{9}$

21) The average of $13, 15, 20$ and x is 18. What is the value of x?

A. 9
B. 15
C. 18
D. 24

22) What is the value of mode and median in the following set of numbers?

$$1, 2, 2, 5, 4, 4, 3, 3, 3, 1, 1$$

A. Mode: $1, 2$ Median: 2
B. Mode: $1, 3$ Median: 3
C. Mode: $2, 3$ Median: 2
D. Mode: $1, 3$ Median: 2.5

23) 5 less than twice a positive integer is 83. What is the integer?

A. 39
B. 41
C. 42
D. 44

24) If Joe was making $\$7.50$ per hour and got a raise to $\$7.75$ per hour, what percentage increase was the raise?

A. 1%
B. 2.67%
C. 3.33%
D. 6.66%

25) Which is the equivalent temperature of $104°F$ in Celsius? ($C = Celsius$)

$$C = \frac{5}{9}(F - 32)$$

A. 32
B. 38
C. 40
D. 44

Quantitative Comparisons

Direction: Questions 26 to 37 are Quantitative Comparisons Questions. Using the information provided in each question, compare the quantity in column A to the quantity in Column B. Choose on your answer sheet grid

A if the quantity in Column A is greater
B if the quantity in Column B is greater
C if the two quantities are equal
D if the relationship cannot be determined from the information given

26) A computer costs $270

Quantity A	Quantity B
A sales tax at 9% of the computer cost	$24.3

27)

Column A	Column B
$3^2 - 5^4$	$3^4 - 5^2$

28) $3x^4 - 45 = 723$

$\frac{1}{5}y - \frac{4}{10} = \frac{3}{5}$

Column A	Column B
x	y

29)

Column A	Column B
$\frac{\sqrt{81-49}}{\sqrt{16-9}}$	$\frac{(9-7)}{(4-3)}$

30)

Column A	Column B
$\sqrt{25} - \sqrt{9}$	$\sqrt{25 - 9}$

31) The sum of 3 consecutive integers is 54.

Column A	Column B
The largest of these integers	20

32)

Column A	Column B
The slope of the line $-4x + 4y = 1$	The slope of the line that passes through points $(3, 5)$ and $(1, 3)$

33) 10 percent of x is equal to 8 percent of y, where x and y are positive numbers.

Quantity A	Quantity B
x	y

34)

Quantity A	Quantity B
$(-4)^3$	4^3

35)

Quantity A	Quantity B
The least prime factor of 22	The least prime factor of 32

36)

Quantity A	Quantity B
$(1.25)^2(1.25)^6$	$(1.25)^8$

37) x is a positive number.

Quantity A	Quantity B
x^6	x^{11}

IF YOU FINISH BEFORE TIME IS CALLED, YOU MAY CHECK YOUR WORK ON THIS SECTION ONLY. DO NOT TURN TO OTHER SECTION IN THE TEST.

STOP

ISEE Middle Level Math

Practice Test 4

Section 2

47 questions

Total time for this section: 40 Minutes

You may NOT use a calculator for this test.

1) If $x =$ lowest common multiple of 30 and 35, then $\frac{x}{2} + 1$ equal to?
A. 210
B. 108
C. 106
D. 96

2) What is the value of x in the following equation?

$$3^x - 15 = 66$$

A. 3
B. 4
C. 5
D. 6

3) Which of the following is not synonym for10^2?
A. 10 cubed
B. 10 squared
C. The square of 10
D. 10 to the second power

4) If angles A , B and C are angles of a parallelogram, what is the sum of the measures of the three angles?
A. $360\ degrees$
B. $180\ degrees$
C. $90\ degrees$
D. Cannot be determined

5) A swing moves from one extreme point (point A) to the opposite extreme point (point B) in 30 seconds. How long does it take that the swing moves 10 times from point A to point B and returns to point A?
A. $600\ seconds$
B. $300\ seconds$
C. $200\ seconds$
D. $100\ seconds$

6) There are 2 cars moving in the same direction on a road. A red car is $10\ km$ ahead of a blue car. If the speed of the red car is $50\ km\ per\ hour$ and the speed of the blue car is $1\frac{2}{5}$ of the red car, how many minutes will it take the blue car to catch the red car?
A. 8.5
B. 15
C. 30
D. 60

7) If the area of trapezoid is 100, what is the perimeter of the trapezoid?

A. 25
B. 28
C. 35
D. 45

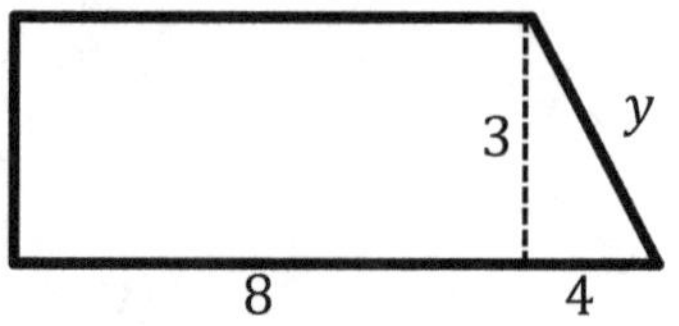

8) In two successive years, the population of a town is increased by 15% and 20%. What percent of the population is increased after two years?

A. 32%
B. 35%
C. 38%
D. 42%

9) In 1999, the average worker's income increased \$2,000 per year starting from \$24,000 annual salary. Which equation represents income greater than average? ($I =$ income, $x =$ number of years after 1999)

A. $I > 2{,}000x + 24{,}000$
B. $I > -2{,}000x + 24{,}000$
C. $I < -2{,}000x + 24{,}000$
D. $I < 2{,}000x - 24{,}000$

10) Which of the following angles is obtuse?

A. $220\ degrees$
B. $340\ degrees$
C. $79\ degrees$
D. $110\ degrees$

11) $8 + 7 \times (-2) - [5 + 22 \times 4] \div 6 = ?$

A. 120
B. 88
C. -21.5
D. -20

12) What is ratio of perimeter of figure A to area of figure B?

A. $\frac{3}{8}$
B. $\frac{8}{3}$
C. $\frac{8}{5}$
D. $\frac{5}{8}$

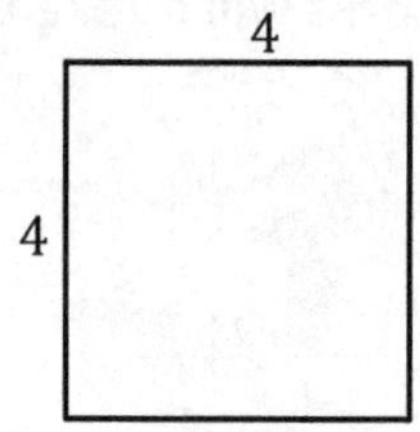

Fig. A

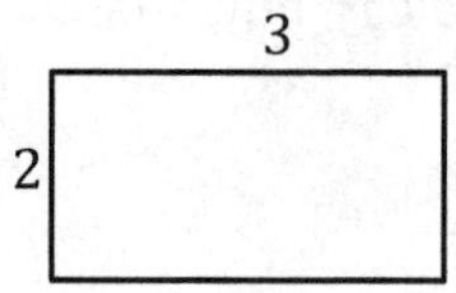

Fig. B

13) Mr. Jones saves \$2,500 out of his monthly family income of \$55,000. What fractional part of his income does he save?

A. $\frac{1}{22}$
B. $\frac{1}{11}$
C. $\frac{3}{25}$
D. $\frac{2}{15}$

14) Anita's trick–or–treat bag contains 12 pieces of chocolate, 18 suckers, 18 pieces of gum, 24 pieces of licorice. If she randomly pulls a piece of candy from her bag, what is the probability of her pulling out a piece of sucker

A. $\frac{1}{3}$
B. $\frac{1}{4}$
C. $\frac{1}{6}$
D. $\frac{1}{12}$

15) What is the difference in area between a $9\ cm$ by $4\ cm$ rectangle and a circle with diameter of $10\ cm$? ($\pi = 3$)

A. 49
B. 40
C. 39
D. 26

16) What is the value (values) of x in the following equation?

$$(x^2 + 4x + 4) = 100$$

A. $-8, 12$
B. $8, -12$
C. -8
D. 12

17) 120 is equal to?

A. $20 - (4 \times 10) + (6 \times 30)$
B. $\left(\frac{11}{8} \times 72\right) + \left(\frac{125}{5}\right)$
C. $\left(\left(\frac{30}{4} + \frac{13}{2}\right) \times 7\right) - \frac{11}{2} + \frac{110}{4}$
D. $(2 \times 10) + (50 \times 1.5) + 15$

18) $\frac{15 \times 21}{8}$ is closest estimate to?

A. 39.4
B. 40.5
C. 42.6
D. 45.2

19) When a number is multiplied to itself and added by 10, the result is 35. What is the value of the number?

A. 5 and -5
B. 6 and -6
C. 5
D. 6

20) If Tom invests \$1,000 at an annual rate of 4.5%, how much interest will he earn after two year?

A. \$9,000
B. \$4,500
C. \$900
D. \$90

21) How many possible outfit combinations come from six shirts, three slacks, and five ties?

A. 90
B. 60
C. 15
D. 14

22) What is the value of x in the equation $\frac{x}{8} + \frac{5}{8} = \frac{15}{4}$?

A. 25
B. 15
C. 8
D. 5

23) What is the absolute value of the quantity six minus nine?

A. -3
B. 15
C. -15
D. 3

24) If $y = 4ab + 3b^3$, what is y when $a = 2$ and $b = 3$?
A. 110
B. 105
C. 81
D. 36

25) Which of the following angles can represent the three angles of a triangle?
A. $20°, 80°, 90°$
B. $50°, 50°, 90°$
C. $10°, 110°, 60°$
D. $55°, 45°, 70°$

26) In the following equation, what is the value of $x - 2y$?

$$x + 3x - 10 = 2\left(\frac{3}{2}x + y\right) - 15$$

A. 5
B. -25
C. -5
D. 25

27) Two-kilogram banana and three-kilograms grapes cost $\$28$. If the price of one-kilogram of banana is twice the price of one-kilogram of grape, how much does one kilogram banana cost?
A. $\$8$
B. $\$4$
C. $\$2$
D. $\$1$

28) Which is **NOT** a prime number?
A. 29
B. 43
C. 47
D. 121

29) How many tiles of $8\ cm^2$ is needed to cover a floor of dimension $6\ cm$ by $24\ cm$?
A. 12
B. 18
C. 24
D. 36

30) There are three books, a red book, a blue book, and a white book. If the weight of the red book is $80\ g$ and it is 40% of the weight of the blue book, and the weight of the blue book is 125% of the weight of the white book, what is the weight of all three books?

A. $400\ g$
B. $300\ g$
C. $250\ g$
D. $200\ g$

31) Each of the x students in a team may invite up to 5 friends to a party. What is the maximum number of students and guests who might attend the party?

A. $5x + 5$
B. $5x$
C. $x + 5$
D. $6x$

32) Calculate the approximate circumference of the following circle. (diameter is 20)

A. $1{,}257$
B. 314
C. 63
D. 56

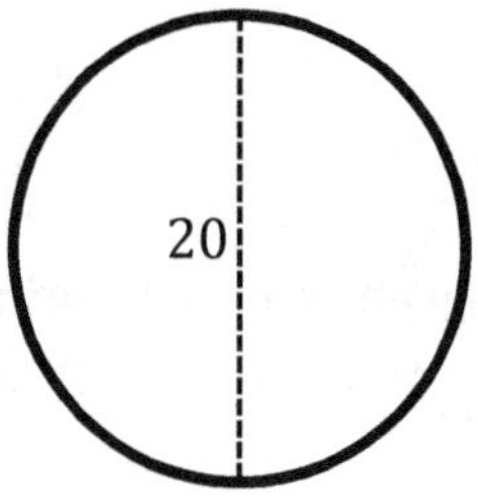

33) $270\ minutes = \cdots ?$

A. $5\ Hours$
B. $4.5\ Hours$
C. $3.5\ Hours$
D. $0.2\ Hours$

34) In the figure below, two lines are parallel. What is the value of angle x?

A. $35\ degree$
B. $92\ degree$
C. $120\ degree$
D. $145\ degree$

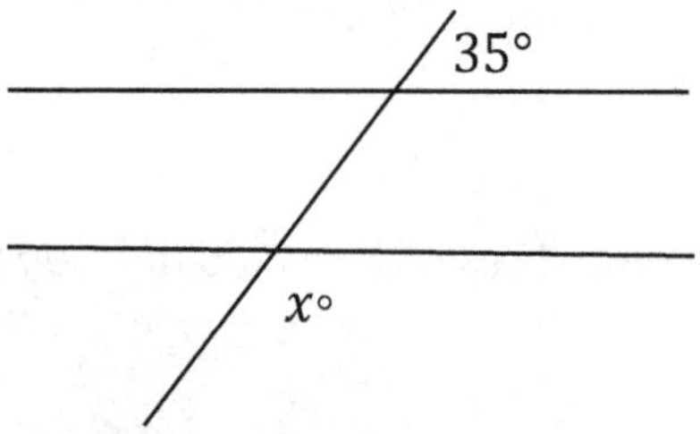

35) $\left(\left((-25) + 50\right) \times \frac{1}{5}\right) + (-10)?$

A. 5
B. 6
C. -5
D. -6

36) Adam drove 340 miles and it took him approximately 8 hours. How many miles per hour was his average speed?

A. about 44.5 miles per hour
B. about 42.5 miles per hour
C. about 36.5 miles per hour
D. about 31.5 miles per hour

37) Three people go to a restaurant. Their bill comes to $56.00. They decided to split the cost. One person pays $8.5, the next person pays 2 times that amount. How much will the third person have to pay?

A. $36.50
B. $30.50
C. $25.00
D. $20.00

38) What is 21,8210 in scientific notation?

A. 218.21×10^3
B. 21.821×10^4
C. 0.21821×10^6
D. 2.1821×10^5

39) What is the perimeter of the below right triangle?

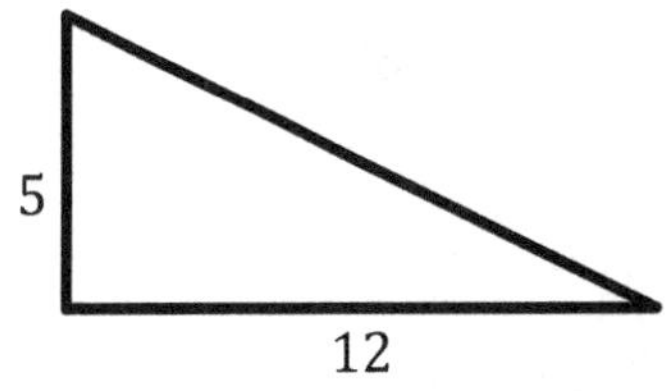

A. 60
B. 30
C. 20
D. 10

40) If 120% of a number is equal to 25% of 90, then what is the number?

A. 22.75
B. 18.75
C. 12.75
D. 10.75

41) What is the value of $(12 - 8)!$?

A. 20
B. 24
C. 27
D. 28

42) If x represents the greatest even multiple odd 11 less than 80, and y represents the least odd multiple of 9 greater than 30, what is $x + y$?
A. 111
B. 113
C. 122
D. 145

43) The average weight of 20 girls in a class is 50 kg and the average weight of 30 boys in the same class is 60 kg. What is the average weight of all the 50 students in that class?
A. 56 kg
B. 58 kg
C. 59 kg
D. 59.5 kg

44) What is x in the following right triangle?

A. $\sqrt{388}$
B. 20
C. $\sqrt{401}$
D. 22

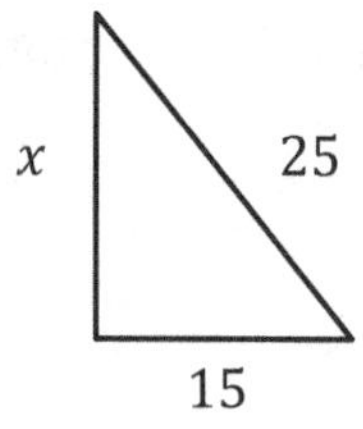

45) John traveled 150 km in 6 hours and Alice traveled 180 km in 4 hours. What is the ratio of the average speed of John to average speed of Alice?
A. 3 : 2
B. 2 : 3
C. 5 : 9
D. 5 : 6

46) An angle is equal to one fifth of its supplement. What is the measure of that angle?
A. 20
B. 30
C. 45
D. 60

47) What is the difference of smallest 4–digit number and biggest 4–digit number?

A. 6,666
B. 6,789
C. 8,888
D. 8,999

IF YOU FINISH BEFORE TIME IS CALLED, YOU MAY CHECK YOUR WORK ON THIS SECTION.

STOP

ISEE Middle Level Math Practice Test 5

2019 - 2020

Two Parts

Total number of questions: 84

Part 1 (Quantitative Reasoning): 37 questions

Part 2 (Mathematics Achievement): 47 questions

Total time for two parts: 75 Minutes

ISEE Middle Level Practice Test Answer Sheets

Remove (or photocopy) this answer sheet and use it to complete the practice test.

ISEE Middle Level Practice Test 5

Quantitative Reasoning				Mathematics Achievement			
1	Ⓐ Ⓑ Ⓒ Ⓓ	25	Ⓐ Ⓑ Ⓒ Ⓓ	1	Ⓐ Ⓑ Ⓒ Ⓓ	25	Ⓐ Ⓑ Ⓒ Ⓓ
2	Ⓐ Ⓑ Ⓒ Ⓓ	26	Ⓐ Ⓑ Ⓒ Ⓓ	2	Ⓐ Ⓑ Ⓒ Ⓓ	26	Ⓐ Ⓑ Ⓒ Ⓓ
3	Ⓐ Ⓑ Ⓒ Ⓓ	27	Ⓐ Ⓑ Ⓒ Ⓓ	3	Ⓐ Ⓑ Ⓒ Ⓓ	27	Ⓐ Ⓑ Ⓒ Ⓓ
4	Ⓐ Ⓑ Ⓒ Ⓓ	28	Ⓐ Ⓑ Ⓒ Ⓓ	4	Ⓐ Ⓑ Ⓒ Ⓓ	28	Ⓐ Ⓑ Ⓒ Ⓓ
5	Ⓐ Ⓑ Ⓒ Ⓓ	29	Ⓐ Ⓑ Ⓒ Ⓓ	5	Ⓐ Ⓑ Ⓒ Ⓓ	29	Ⓐ Ⓑ Ⓒ Ⓓ
6	Ⓐ Ⓑ Ⓒ Ⓓ	30	Ⓐ Ⓑ Ⓒ Ⓓ	6	Ⓐ Ⓑ Ⓒ Ⓓ	30	Ⓐ Ⓑ Ⓒ Ⓓ
7	Ⓐ Ⓑ Ⓒ Ⓓ	31	Ⓐ Ⓑ Ⓒ Ⓓ	7	Ⓐ Ⓑ Ⓒ Ⓓ	31	Ⓐ Ⓑ Ⓒ Ⓓ
8	Ⓐ Ⓑ Ⓒ Ⓓ	32	Ⓐ Ⓑ Ⓒ Ⓓ	8	Ⓐ Ⓑ Ⓒ Ⓓ	32	Ⓐ Ⓑ Ⓒ Ⓓ
9	Ⓐ Ⓑ Ⓒ Ⓓ	33	Ⓐ Ⓑ Ⓒ Ⓓ	9	Ⓐ Ⓑ Ⓒ Ⓓ	33	Ⓐ Ⓑ Ⓒ Ⓓ
10	Ⓐ Ⓑ Ⓒ Ⓓ	34	Ⓐ Ⓑ Ⓒ Ⓓ	10	Ⓐ Ⓑ Ⓒ Ⓓ	34	Ⓐ Ⓑ Ⓒ Ⓓ
11	Ⓐ Ⓑ Ⓒ Ⓓ	35	Ⓐ Ⓑ Ⓒ Ⓓ	11	Ⓐ Ⓑ Ⓒ Ⓓ	35	Ⓐ Ⓑ Ⓒ Ⓓ
12	Ⓐ Ⓑ Ⓒ Ⓓ	36	Ⓐ Ⓑ Ⓒ Ⓓ	12	Ⓐ Ⓑ Ⓒ Ⓓ	36	Ⓐ Ⓑ Ⓒ Ⓓ
13	Ⓐ Ⓑ Ⓒ Ⓓ	37	Ⓐ Ⓑ Ⓒ Ⓓ	13	Ⓐ Ⓑ Ⓒ Ⓓ	37	Ⓐ Ⓑ Ⓒ Ⓓ
14	Ⓐ Ⓑ Ⓒ Ⓓ			14	Ⓐ Ⓑ Ⓒ Ⓓ	38	Ⓐ Ⓑ Ⓒ Ⓓ
15	Ⓐ Ⓑ Ⓒ Ⓓ			15	Ⓐ Ⓑ Ⓒ Ⓓ	39	Ⓐ Ⓑ Ⓒ Ⓓ
16	Ⓐ Ⓑ Ⓒ Ⓓ			16	Ⓐ Ⓑ Ⓒ Ⓓ	40	Ⓐ Ⓑ Ⓒ Ⓓ
17	Ⓐ Ⓑ Ⓒ Ⓓ			17	Ⓐ Ⓑ Ⓒ Ⓓ	41	Ⓐ Ⓑ Ⓒ Ⓓ
18	Ⓐ Ⓑ Ⓒ Ⓓ			18	Ⓐ Ⓑ Ⓒ Ⓓ	42	Ⓐ Ⓑ Ⓒ Ⓓ
19	Ⓐ Ⓑ Ⓒ Ⓓ			19	Ⓐ Ⓑ Ⓒ Ⓓ	43	Ⓐ Ⓑ Ⓒ Ⓓ
20	Ⓐ Ⓑ Ⓒ Ⓓ			20	Ⓐ Ⓑ Ⓒ Ⓓ	44	Ⓐ Ⓑ Ⓒ Ⓓ
21	Ⓐ Ⓑ Ⓒ Ⓓ			21	Ⓐ Ⓑ Ⓒ Ⓓ	45	Ⓐ Ⓑ Ⓒ Ⓓ
22	Ⓐ Ⓑ Ⓒ Ⓓ			22	Ⓐ Ⓑ Ⓒ Ⓓ	46	Ⓐ Ⓑ Ⓒ Ⓓ
23	Ⓐ Ⓑ Ⓒ Ⓓ			23	Ⓐ Ⓑ Ⓒ Ⓓ	47	Ⓐ Ⓑ Ⓒ Ⓓ
24	Ⓐ Ⓑ Ⓒ Ⓓ			24	Ⓐ Ⓑ Ⓒ Ⓓ		

ISEE Middle Level Math

Practice Test 5

Section 1

37 questions

Total time for this section: 35 Minutes

You may NOT use a calculator for this test.

1) Which of the following shows the numbers in increasing order?
A. $\frac{1}{6}, \frac{2}{5}, \frac{1}{3}, \frac{3}{4}$
B. $\frac{1}{6}, \frac{2}{5}, \frac{3}{4}, \frac{1}{3}$
C. $\frac{1}{6}, \frac{1}{3}, \frac{2}{5}, \frac{3}{4}$
D. $\frac{1}{6}, \frac{3}{4}, \frac{1}{3}, \frac{2}{5}$

2) $452{,}357{,}841 \times 0.0001$?
A. $452{,}357.841$
B. $45{,}235.7841$
C. $4{,}523.57841$
D. 452.357841

3) Jim purchased a table for 20% off and saved $\$23$. What was the original price of the table?
A. $\$90$
B. $\$100$
C. $\$115$
D. 140

4) A $\$40$ shirt now selling for $\$28$ is discounted by what percent?
A. 20%
B. 30%
C. 40%
D. 60%

5) If $f = 2x - 3y$ and $g = x + 4y$, what is $2f + g$?
A. $3x - y$
B. $3x - 2y$
C. $5x - 2y$
D. $5x - y$

6) What is the value of $\frac{-58 \times 0.5}{4}$?
A. -16
B. -7.25
C. 7.25
D. 16

7) What is the value of x in the following equation? $8^x = 512$
A. 7
B. 5
C. 4
D. 3

8) The score of Emma was half as that of Ava and the score of Mia was twice that of Ava. If the score of Mia was 60, what is the score of Emma?

A. 15
B. 18
C. 20
D. 30

9) The area of a circle is $64\ \pi$. What is the circumference of the circle?

A. $8\ \pi$
B. $16\ \pi$
C. $32\ \pi$
D. $64\ \pi$

10) Round off the result of 1.12×7.2 to the nearest tenth?

A. 7
B. 8
C. 8.06
D. 8.1

11) What is the value of x in the following figure?

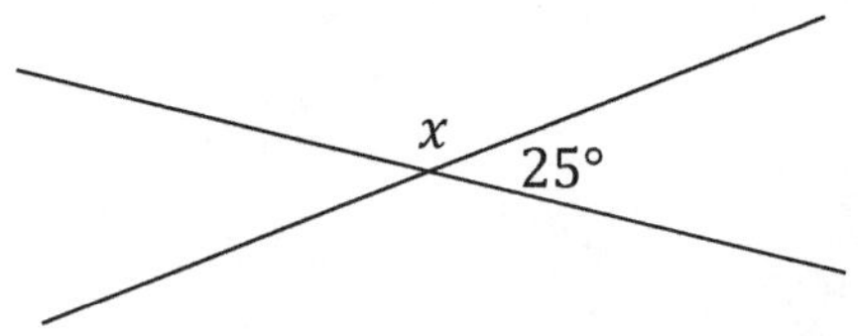

A. $25°$
B. $65°$
C. $115°$
D. $155°$

12) Two third of 18 is equal to $\frac{2}{5}$ of what number?

A. 60
B. 40
C. 35
D. 30

13) In five successive hours, a car traveled $40\ km$, $45\ km$, $50\ km$, $35\ km$ and $65\ km$. In the next five hours, it traveled with an average speed of $50\ km\ per\ hour$. Find the total distance the car traveled in 10 hours.

A. $425\ km$
B. $450\ km$
C. $485\ km$
D. $500\ km$

14) What is the mean in the following set of numbers?

$$9, 12, 29, 36, 45, 63, 99, 123$$

A. 46.2
B. 40.5
C. 59.4
D. 52

15) The perimeter of the trapezoid below is 60. What is its area?

A. $252\ cm^2$
B. $234\ cm^2$
C. $216\ cm^2$
D. $208\ cm^2$

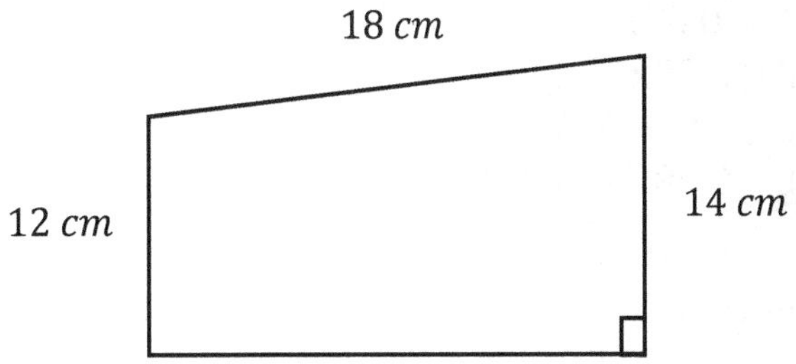

16) The price of a laptop is decreased by 10% to $\$360$. What is its original price?
A. $\$320$
B. $\$380$
C. $\$390$
D. $\$400$

17) Find $\frac{1}{4}$ of $\frac{2}{5}$ of 120?
A. 16
B. 12
C. 8
D. 4

18) The ratio of boys and girls in a class is $4:7$. If there are 66 students in the class, how many more boys should be enrolled to make the ratio $1:1$?
A. 8
B. 10
C. 18
D. 20

19) What is the value of x in the following equation?

$$5(x+1) = 15(x-4) + 25$$

A. 12
B. 4
C. 3.2
D. 2.5

20) A company pays its employee $\$5{,}000$ plus 2% of all sales profit. If x is all sold profit, which of the following represents the employee's revenue?

A. $0.02x$
B. $0.98x - 5{,}000$
C. $0.02x + 5{,}000$
D. $0.98x + 5{,}000$

21) Which of the following is a correct statement?

A. $\frac{3}{4} > 0.8$
B. $10\% = \frac{2}{5}$
C. $3 < \frac{5}{2}$
D. $\frac{5}{6} > 0.8$

22) What is the value of x in the following figure?

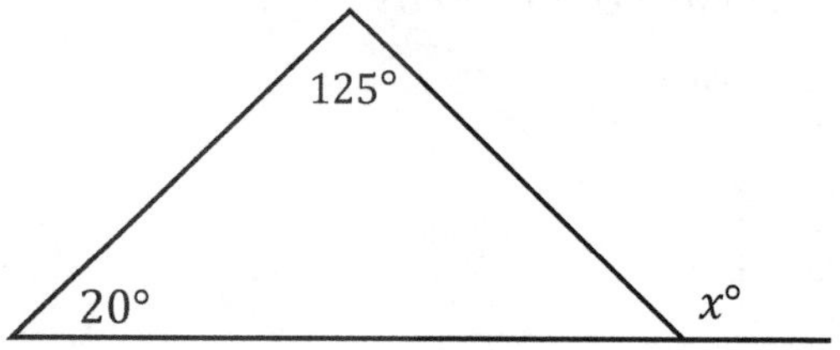

A. 150
B. 145
C. 125
D. 105

23) What is the area of a square whose diagonal is 8?

A. 16
B. 32
C. 36
D. 64

24) What is value of $-26 - (-65)$?

A. 39
B. -91
C. -39
D. 91

25) Car A use 8-liter petrol per 100 kilometers; car B use 6-liter petrol per 100 kilometers. If both cars drive 250 kilometers, how much more petrol does car A use?

A. 5
B. 10
C. 15
D. 20

Quantitative Comparisons

Direction: Questions 26 to 37 are Quantitative Comparisons Questions. Using the information provided in each question, compare the quantity in column A to the quantity in Column B. Choose on your answer sheet grid

A if the quantity in Column A is greater
B if the quantity in Column B is greater
C if the two quantities are equal
D if the relationship cannot be determined from the information given

26)

Column A	Column B
$6 + 4 \times 7 + 8$	$4 + 6 \times 7 - 8$

27) $y = -4x - 8$

Column A	Column B
The value of x when $y = 12$	-4

28)

Column A	Column B
$\sqrt{36} + \sqrt{36}$	$\sqrt{72}$

29) The average age of Joe, Michelle, and Nicole is 32.

Column A	Column B
The average age of Joe and Michelle	The average age of Michelle and Nicole

30)

Column A	**Column B**
$\sqrt{121-64}$	$\sqrt{121}-\sqrt{64}$

31) A right cylinder with radius 4 inches has volume 160π cubic inches.

Quantity A	Quantity B
The height of the cylinder	9.8 inches

32) x is an integer greater than zero.

Quantity A	Quantity B
$\frac{1}{x}+x$	8

33)

$$\frac{4}{5}<x<\frac{6}{7}$$

Quantity A	Quantity B
x	$\frac{5}{6}$

34) x is an integer.

Quantity A	Quantity B
$\frac{x^6}{6}$	$(\frac{x}{6})^6$

35) The ratio of blue to black marbles in a basket is 3 to 10.

Quantity A	Quantity B
Twice the number of blue marbles in the basket	Half the number of black marbles in the basket

36) a and b are real numbers.

$$a < b$$

Quantity A	Quantity B
$\lvert a - b \rvert$	$\lvert b - a \rvert$

37) $2x^3 + 10 = 64$
$120 - 18y = 84$

Quantity A	Quantity B
x	y

IF YOU FINISH BEFORE TIME IS CALLED, YOU MAY CHECK YOUR WORK ON THIS SECTION ONLY. DO NOT TURN TO ANY OTHER SECTION IN THE TEST. STOP

ISEE Middle Level Math

Practice Test 5

Section 2

47 questions

Total time for this section: 40 Minutes

You may NOT use a calculator for this test.

1) What number is 12 more than 15% of 180?
A. 40
B. 39
C. 15
D. 10

2) If the number of red cars to blue cars in a parking lot is in the ratio of 2: 5, how many red cars are there if 90 blue cars are in the parking lot?
A. 72
B. 36
C. 25
D. 10

3) $3\left(\frac{1}{3}-\frac{1}{9}\right)+1?$
A. 1.5
B. 1.66 ...
C. 5.5
D. 5.11 ...

4) In a bundle of 90 pencils, 43 are red and the rest are blue. About what percent of the bundle is composed of blue pencils?
A. 62%
B. 58%
C. 54%
D. 52%

5) Which of the following is one value of x in the following equation?

$$(x+5)^2 = 144$$

A. 1
B. −17
C. −1
D. −7

6) What number is 7 less than 50% of 36?
A. 10
B. 11
C. 18
D. 23

7) Which is equivalent to the following equation? $x = \frac{2y}{3} - 6$

A. $2y - 3x - 18 = 0$
B. $2x + 3x = -6$
C. $3x + 6 = \frac{2y}{3}$
D. $3x - 2y = -6$

8) The price of a car was $20,000 in 2014, $16,000 in 2015 and $12,800 in 2016. What is the rate of depreciation of the price of car per year?

A. 15%
B. 20%
C. 25%
D. 30%

9) When a number is subtracted from 24 and the difference is divided by that number, the result is 3. What is the value of the number?

A. 2
B. 4
C. 6
D. 12

10) 95 is equal to?

A. $2 + (3 \times 10) + (2 \times 30)$
B. $\left(\frac{10}{3} \times 27\right) + (\frac{5}{2} \times 2)$
C. $(\left(\frac{3}{2} + 3\right) \times \frac{18}{3}) + 63$
D. $(2 \times 15) + (50 \times 2) - 46$

11) If $\frac{3x}{2} = 60$, then $\frac{2x}{5} = ?$

A. 16
B. 20
C. 25
D. 30

12) Which of the following is the greatest number?

A. $\frac{1}{3}$
B. $\frac{7}{9}$
C. 0.9
D. 85%

13) The surface of a cube is $150\ cm^2$. What is the volume of the cube?

A. $175\ cm^3$
B. $125\ cm^3$
C. $90\ cm^3$
D. $25\ cm^3$

14) If 150% of a number is 60, then what is the 90% of that number?
A. 36
B. 50
C. 70
D. 85

15) What is the missing term in the given numbers?

$$2, 3, 5, 8, 12, 17, 23, \_\_, 38$$

A. 24
B. 26
C. 27
D. 30

16) Which of the following angles can represent the three angles of an isosceles right triangle?
A. $10°, 80°, 90°$
B. $50°, 50°, 80°$
C. $60°, 60°, 60°$
D. $45°, 45°, 90°$

17) What is the value of the expression $0.45 + 0.3 + 2.6 + 2.94$?
A. 5.78
B. 6.02
C. 6.29
D. 8.33

18) When a gas tank can hold 25 gallons, how many gallons does it contain when it is $\frac{2}{5}$ full?
A. 125
B. 62.5
C. 50
D. 10

19) Which graph does not represent y as a function of x?

A.

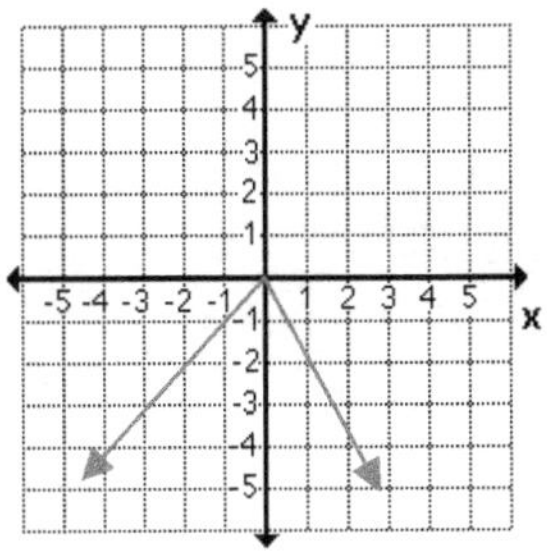

B.

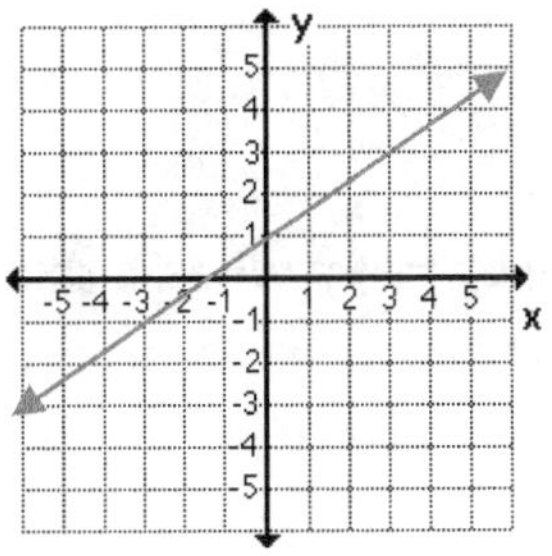

C.

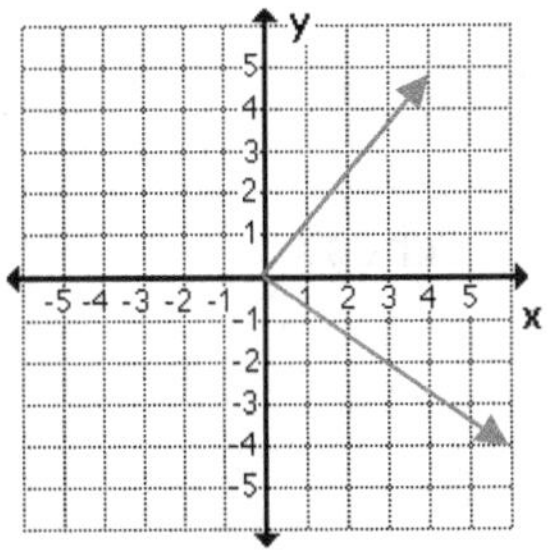

D.

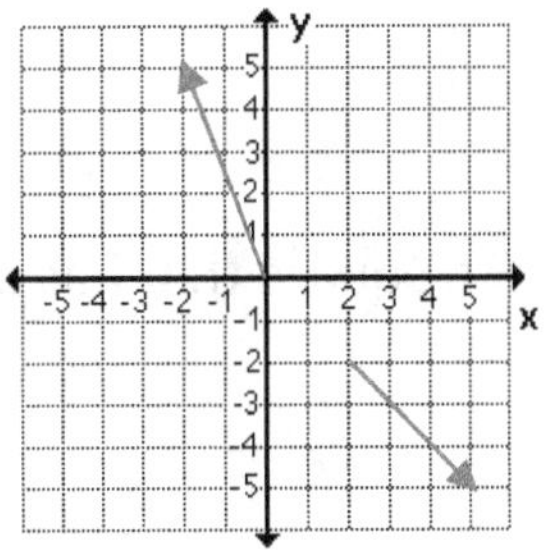

20) Which of the following is equivalent to $13 < -3x - 2 < 22$?

A. $-8 < x < -5$
B. $5 < x < 8$
C. $\frac{11}{3} < x < \frac{20}{3}$
D. $\frac{-20}{3} < x < \frac{-11}{3}$

21) In a certain bookshelf of a library, there are 35 biology books, 95 history books, and 80 language books. What is the ratio of the number of biology books to the total number of books in this bookshelf?

A. $\frac{1}{4}$
B. $\frac{1}{6}$
C. $\frac{2}{7}$
D. $\frac{3}{8}$

22) $185\ minutes\ = ...?$
A. $3.25\ hours$
B. $3.08\ hours$
C. $2\ hours$
D. $1.8\ hours$

23) In the equation $2x - 12 + 4 = 4y$ what is the value of $(2y - x)$?
A. 16
B. 8
C. -4
D. -8

24) Which of the following is **NOT** a prime number?
A. 103
B. 97
C. 79
D. 57

25) What is the perimeter of a square that has an area of 64 square inches?
A. $144\ inches$
B. $64\ inches$
C. $32\ inches$
D. $16\ inches$

26) Jason left a $\$12.00$ tip on a lunch that cost $\$48.00$, approximately what percentage was the tip?
A. 2.5%
B. 10%
C. 15%
D. 25%

27) Two-kilograms apple and three-kilograms orange cost $\$26.4$. If one-kilogram apple costs $\$4.2$ how much does one-kilogram orange cost?
A. $\$9$
B. $\$6$
C. $\$5.5$
D. $\$5$

28) $\Big(\big((-12) + 20\big) \times 2\Big) + (-15)$?
A. 1
B. 2
C. 3
D. 8

29) The width of a rectangle is $4x$ and its length is $6x$. The perimeter of the rectangle is 80. What is the value of x?

A. 4
B. 5
C. 6
D. 10

30) Jason is 9 miles ahead of Joe running at 5.5 miles per hour and Joe is running at the speed of 7 miles per hour. How long does it take Joe to catch Jason?

A. $3\ hours$
B. $4\ hours$
C. $6\ hours$
D. $8\ hours$

31) $[5 \times (-14) + 8] - (-4) + [4 \times 5] \div 2 = ?$

A. 144
B. 48
C. -144
D. -48

32) If 40% of a class are girls, and 25% of girls play tennis, what percent of the class play tennis?

A. 10%
B. 15%
C. 20%
D. 40%

33) In a class, there are twice as many girls as boys. If the total number of students in the class is 48, how many girls are in the class?

A. 16
B. 24
C. 32
D. 36

34) At a Zoo, the ratio of lions to tigers is 5 to 3. Which of the following could NOT be the total number of lions and tigers in the zoo?

A. 64
B. 80
C. 98
D. 112

35) The price of a sofa is decreased by 25% to $\$420$. What was its original price?
A. $\$480$
B. $\$550$
C. $\$560$
D. $\$600$

36) A shaft rotates 300 times in 8 seconds. How many times does it rotate in 12 seconds?
A. 450
B. 300
C. 200
D. 100

37) What is the value of x in the equation $10x - 15.5 = -45.5$?
A. -3
B. -2
C. 2
D. 3

38) A swimming pool holds $2{,}000$ cubic feet of water. The swimming pool is 25 feet long and 10 feet wide. How deep is the swimming pool?
A. $2\ feet$
B. $4\ feet$
C. $6\ feet$
D. $8\ feet$

39) What is the value of x the following equation?

$$6^x = 1{,}296$$

A. 3
B. 4
C. 5
D. 6

40) What is the area of the trapezoid?
A. 25
B. 50
C. 100
D. 200

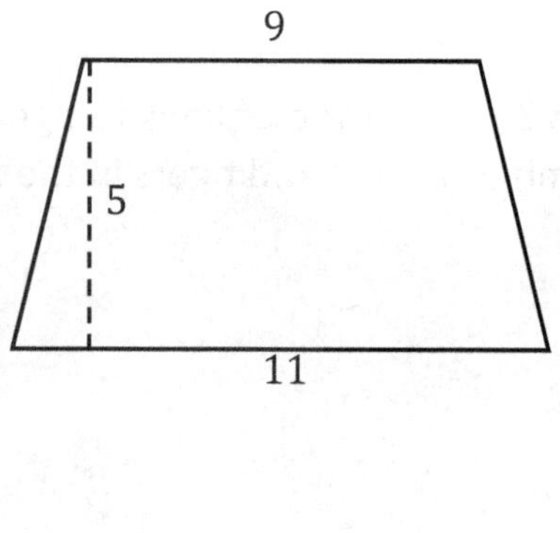

41) $12.124 \div 0.002$?
A. 6.062
B. 60.62
C. 606.2
D. $6{,}062$

42) What is the value of x in the following equation?

$$10 + 4(x + 5 - 5x) = 30$$

A. 0
B. 1
C. 2
D. 3

43) Ella bought a pair of gloves for $\$12.49$. She gave the clerk $\$18.00$. How much change should she get back?

A. $\$4.51$
B. $\$5.51$
C. $\$6.51$
D. $\$7.51$

44) If 60% of A is 20% of B, then B is what percent of A?

A. 3%
B. 30%
C. 200%
D. 300%

45) A card is drawn at random from a standard 52–card deck, what is the probability that the card is of Hearts? (The deck includes 13 of each suit clubs, diamonds, hearts, and spades)

A. $\frac{1}{3}$
B. $\frac{1}{4}$
C. $\frac{1}{6}$
D. $\frac{1}{52}$

46) $\frac{3}{4} + \frac{\frac{-2}{5}}{\frac{4}{10}} = ?$

A. $\frac{1}{4}$
B. $\frac{1}{2}$
C. $-\frac{1}{4}$
D. $-\frac{1}{2}$

47) $\frac{7\times 12}{80}$ is closest estimate to?

A. 0.88

B. 1.1

C. 1.9

D. 2.4

IF YOU FINISH BEFORE TIME IS CALLED, YOU MAY CHECK YOUR WORK ON THIS SECTION ONLY. DO NOT TURN TO ANY OTHER SECTION IN THE TEST. STOP

ISEE Middle Level Math Practice Tests Answers and Explanations

Now, it's time to review your results to see where you went wrong and what areas you need to improve!

ISEE Middle Level Math Practice Test 1 Answer Key

Quantitative Reasoning						Mathematics Achievement					
1	B	17	C	33	D	1	C	17	B	33	D
2	B	18	C	34	D	2	C	18	A	34	A
3	B	19	C	35	C	3	A	19	C	35	C
4	A	20	D	36	A	4	D	20	B	36	A
5	D	21	D	37	D	5	D	21	C	37	A
6	C	22	A			6	B	22	B	38	A
7	B	23	A			7	C	23	D	39	C
8	D	24	A			8	C	24	C	40	B
9	A	25	A			9	A	25	D	41	B
10	B	26	A			10	B	26	D	42	D
11	D	27	B			11	C	27	A	43	B
12	D	28	A			12	D	28	D	44	B
13	C	29	D			13	C	29	B	45	C
14	D	30	A			14	D	30	D	46	C
15	D	31	A			15	B	31	D	47	C
16	B	32	A			16	D	32	A		

ISEE Middle Level Math Practice Test 2 Answer Key

Quantitative Reasoning

1	A	17	C	33	A
2	B	18	A	34	B
3	B	19	A	35	C
4	C	20	C	36	C
5	B	21	A	37	D
6	A	22	D		
7	B	23	D		
8	A	24	D		
9	D	25	B		
10	D	26	A		
11	C	27	B		
12	A	28	A		
13	B	29	C		
14	A	30	C		
15	B	31	C		
16	B	32	A		

Mathematics Achievement

1	A	17	C	33	A
2	A	18	A	34	D
3	D	19	B	35	B
4	D	20	A	36	B
5	B	21	D	37	D
6	B	22	A	38	D
7	D	23	D	39	B
8	D	24	D	40	D
9	C	25	C	41	A
10	A	26	C	42	A
11	D	27	C	43	B
12	A	28	B	44	D
13	B	29	D	45	A
14	D	30	D	46	D
15	D	31	C	47	A
16	B	32	B		

ISEE Middle Level Math Practice Test 3 Answer Key

Quantitative Reasoning						Mathematics Achievement					
1	C	17	B	33	B	1	B	17	C	33	A
2	B	18	C	34	A	2	B	18	D	34	C
3	C	19	B	35	A	3	B	19	A	35	C
4	B	20	C	36	C	4	D	20	C	36	A
5	C	21	D	37	C	5	B	21	C	37	A
6	B	22	B			6	B	22	A	38	D
7	C	23	B			7	A	23	D	39	B
8	A	24	A			8	B	24	D	40	B
9	B	25	A			9	C	25	C	41	D
10	D	26	A			10	A	26	D	42	A
11	D	27	D			11	A	27	B	43	B
12	D	28	A			12	C	28	A	44	D
13	C	29	A			13	B	29	A	45	A
14	D	30	A			14	A	30	C	46	C
15	D	31	A			15	A	31	D	47	B
16	D	32	D			16	D	32	A		

ISEE Middle Level Math Practice Test 4 Answer Key

Quantitative Reasoning

1	B	17	C	33	B
2	B	18	B	34	B
3	B	19	C	35	B
4	D	20	A	36	C
5	A	21	D	37	A
6	B	22	B		
7	A	23	D		
8	A	24	C		
9	D	25	C		
10	C	26	C		
11	D	27	A		
12	A	28	B		
13	B	29	A		
14	A	30	B		
15	C	31	B		
16	A	32	C		

Mathematics Achievement

1	C	17	C	33	B
2	B	18	A	34	D
3	A	19	A	35	C
4	D	20	D	36	B
5	A	21	A	37	B
6	C	22	A	38	D
7	B	23	D	39	B
8	C	24	B	40	B
9	A	25	C	41	B
10	D	26	C	42	A
11	C	27	A	43	A
12	B	28	D	44	B
13	A	29	B	45	C
14	B	30	A	46	B
15	C	31	D	47	D
16	B	32	C		

ISEE Middle Level Math Practice Test 5 Answer Key

Quantitative Reasoning | **Mathematics Achievement**

1	C	17	B	33	D	1	B	17	C	33	A
2	B	18	C	34	A	2	B	18	D	34	C
3	C	19	B	35	C	3	B	19	A	35	C
4	B	20	C	36	C	4	D	20	C	36	A
5	C	21	D	37	A	5	B	21	C	37	A
6	B	22	B			6	B	22	A	38	D
7	D	23	B			7	A	23	D	39	B
8	A	24	A			8	B	24	D	40	B
9	B	25	A			9	C	25	C	41	D
10	D	26	A			10	B	26	D	42	A
11	D	27	B			11	A	27	B	43	B
12	D	28	A			12	C	28	A	44	D
13	C	29	D			13	B	29	A	45	B
14	D	30	A			14	A	30	C	46	C
15	D	31	A			15	D	31	D	47	B
16	D	32	D			16	D	32	A		

Score Your Test

ISEE scores are broken down by its four sections: Verbal Reasoning, Reading Comprehension, Quantitative Reasoning, and Mathematics Achievement. A sum of the three sections is also reported.

For the Middle Level ISEE, the score range is 760 to 940, the lowest possible score a student can earn is 760 and the highest score is 940 for each section. A student receives 1 point for every correct answer. There is no penalty for wrong or skipped questions.

The total scaled score for a Middle Level ISEE test is the sum of the scores for all sections. A student will also receive a percentile score of between 1-99% that compares that student's test scores with those of other test takers of same grade and gender from the past 3 years.

Use the next table to convert ISEE Middle level raw score to scaled score for application to 7th and 8th grade.

ISEE Middle Level Scaled Scores									
Raw Score	Quantitative Reasoning		Mathematics Achievement		Raw Score	Quantitative Reasoning		Mathematics Achievement	
	7th Grade	8th Grade	7th Grade	8th Grade		7th Grade	8th Grade	7th Grade	8th Grade
0	760	760	760	760	26	900	885	885	865
1	770	765	770	765	27	905	890	885	865
2	780	770	780	770	28	910	895	890	870
3	790	775	790	775	29	910	900	890	870
4	800	780	800	780	30	915	905	895	875
5	810	785	810	785	31	920	910	895	875
6	820	790	820	790	32	925	915	900	880
7	825	795	825	795	33	930	920	900	880
8	830	800	830	800	34	930	925	905	885
9	835	805	835	805	35	935	930	905	885
10	840	810	840	810	36	935	935	910	890
11	845	815	845	815	37	940	940	910	890
12	850	820	850	820	38			915	895
13	855	825	855	825	39			920	900
14	860	830	855	830	40			925	905
15	865	835	860	835	41			925	910
16	870	840	860	840	42			930	915
17	875	845	865	840	43			930	920
18	880	845	865	845	44			935	925
19	880	850	870	845	45			935	930
20	885	855	870	850	46			940	935
21	885	860	875	850	47			940	940
22	890	865	875	855					
23	890	870	875	855					
24	895	875	880	860					
25	895	880	880	860					

ISEE Middle LEVEL Math Practice Tests Answers and Explanations

ISEE Middle LEVEL Math Practice Test 1 Section 1

1) Choice B is correct

$\frac{-50\times0.5}{5} = -\frac{50\times\frac{1}{2}}{5} = -\frac{\frac{50}{2}}{5} = -\frac{50}{10} = -5$

2) Choice B is correct

Use the formula for Percent of Change: $\frac{New\ Value - Old\ Value}{Old\ Value} \times 100\%$

$\frac{29-41}{41} \times 100 = -29\%$ (negative sign here means that the new price is less than old price)

3) Choice B is correct

$562{,}357{,}741 \times \frac{1}{10{,}000} = 56235.7741$

4) Choice A is correct

30% off equals $\$24$. Let x be the original price of the table. Then:

$30\%\ of\ x = 24 \rightarrow 0.3x = 24 \rightarrow x = \frac{24}{0.3} = 80$

5) Choice D is correct

$3f = 3 \times (3x - 2y) = 9x - 6y, \quad 3f + g = 9x - 6y + x + 5y = 10x - y$

6) Choice C is correct

$\frac{1}{7} \cong 0.14 \quad \frac{1}{3} \cong 0.33 \quad \frac{3}{5} = 0.6 \quad \frac{3}{4} = 0.75$

7) Choice B is correct

$8^x = 512$, and $512 = 8^3 \rightarrow x = 3$

8) Choice D is correct

Supplementary angles sum up to 180 degrees. x and 35 degrees are supplementary angles. Then: $x = 180° - 35° = 145°$

9) Choice A is correct

If the score of Mia was 40, therefore the score of Ava is 20. Since, the score of Emma was half as that of Ava, therefore, the score of Emma is 10.

10) Choice B is correct

Use the formula of areas of circles. $Area\ of\ a\ circle = \pi r^2 \Rightarrow 49\pi = \pi r^2 \Rightarrow 49 = r^2 \Rightarrow r = 7$, Radius of the circle is 7 Now, use the circumference formula:

Circumference $= 2\pi r = 2\pi\,(7) = 14\,\pi$

11) Choice D is correct

Let x be the number. Write the equation and solve for x. $\frac{2}{3} \times 15 = \frac{5}{2} \times x \Rightarrow \frac{2\times15}{3} = \frac{5x}{2}$, use cross multiplication to solve for x. $2 \times 30 = 5x \times 3 \Rightarrow 60 = 15x \Rightarrow x = 4$

12) Choice D is correct

$1.15 = \frac{115}{100}$ and $8.2 = \frac{82}{10}$ $\rightarrow 1.15 \times 8.2 = \frac{115}{100} \times \frac{82}{10} = \frac{9{,}430}{1{,}000} = 9.43 \cong 9.4$

13) Choice C is correct

The perimeter of the trapezoid is 54.

Therefore, the missing side (height) is $= 54 - 17 - 12 - 13 = 12$

Area of the trapezoid: $A = \frac{1}{2}\,h\,(b_1 + b_2) = \frac{1}{2}\,(12)\,(12 + 13) = 150$

14) Choice D is correct

Add the first 5 numbers. $42 + 46 + 52 + 35 + 58 = 233$

To find the distance traveled in the next 5 hours, multiply the average by number of hours.

$Distance = Average \times Rate = 60 \times 5 = 300$, Add both numbers. $300 + 233 = 533$

15) Choice D is correct

$$average = \frac{10 + 13 + 29 + 37 + 46 + 66 + 100 + 124}{8} = 53.12$$

16) Choice B is correct

$\frac{2}{5}$ of $145 = \frac{2}{5} \times 145 = 58$, $\frac{1}{2}$ of $58 = \frac{1}{2} \times 58 = 29$

17) Choice C is correct

Let x be the original price. If the price of a laptop is decreased by 20% to \$320, then: 80% of $x = 320 \Rightarrow 0.80x = 320 \Rightarrow x = 320 \div 0.80 = 400$

18) Choice C is correct

Let x be the sales profit. Then, 3% of sales profit is $0.03x$. Employee's revenue: $0.03x + 7{,}500$

19) Choice C is correct

The ratio of boy to girls is $7:4$. Therefore, there are 7 boys out of 11 students. To find the answer, first divide the total number of students by 11, then multiply the result by 7.

$44 \div 11 = 4 \Rightarrow 4 \times 7 = 28$, There are 28 boys and 16 $(44 - 28)$ girls. So, 12 more girls should be enrolled to make the ratio $1:1$

20) Choice D is correct

Let's review the choices:

A. $\frac{3}{5} > 0.8$ This is not a correct statement. Because $\frac{3}{5} = 0.6$ and it's less than 0.8.

B. $12\% = \frac{2}{5}$ This is not a correct statement. Because $12\% = 0.12$ and $\frac{2}{5} = 0.4$

C. $3 < \frac{5}{2}$ This is not a correct statement. Because $\frac{5}{2} = 2.5$ and it's less than 3.

D. $\frac{7}{6} > 0.8$ This is a correct statement. $\frac{7}{6} = 1.16 \rightarrow 0.8 < \frac{7}{6}$

21) Choice D is correct

Simplify: $6(x+1) = 4(x-4) + 20,\ 6x + 6 = 4x - 16 + 20,\ 6x + 6 = 4x + 4$

Subtract $4x$ from both sides: $2x + 6 = 4$, Add 4 to both sides: $-2 = 2x, \quad -1 = x$

22) Choice A is correct

$x = 25 + 135 = 160$

23) Choice A is correct

Petrol of car A in 350 $km = \frac{4\times350}{140} = 10$, Petrol of car B in $350km = \frac{3\times350}{140} = 7.5,\ 10 - 7.5 = 2.5$

24) Choice A is correct

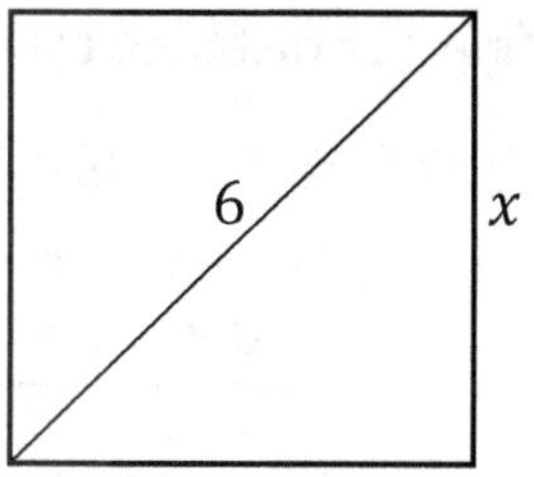

The diagonal of the square is 6. Let x be the side.

Use Pythagorean Theorem: $a^2 + b^2 = c^2$

$x^2 + x^2 = 6^2 \Rightarrow 2x^2 = 6^2 \Rightarrow 2x^2 = 36 \Rightarrow x^2 = 18 \Rightarrow x = \sqrt{18}$

The area of the square is: $\sqrt{18} \times \sqrt{18} = 18$

25) Choice A is correct

$-25 - (-66) = -25 + 66 = 66 - 25 = 41$

26) Choice A is correct.

Column A: Simplify. $\sqrt{36} + \sqrt{36} = 6 + 6 = 12$, 12 is greater than $\sqrt{72}$ ($\sqrt{144} = 12$)

27) Choice B is correct.

Column A: The value of x when $y = 12$:

$y = -4x - 8 \rightarrow 12 = -4x - 8 \rightarrow -4x = 20 \rightarrow x = -5$

Column B: -4, -4 is greater than -5.

28) Choice A is correct.

Column A: Use order of operation to calculate the result.

$6 + 4 \times 7 + 8 = 6 + 28 + 8 = 42$

Column B: $4 + 6 \times 7 - 8 \rightarrow 4 + 42 - 8 = 38$

29) Choice D is correct.

Column A: Based on information provided, we cannot find the average age of Joe and Michelle or average age of Michelle and Nicole.

30) Choice A is correct.

Column A: Simplify.$\sqrt{121-64}=\sqrt{57}$

Column B: $\sqrt{121}-\sqrt{64}=11-8=3$, $\sqrt{57}$ is bigger than 3. ($\sqrt{9}=3$)

31) Choice A is correct

Volume of a right cylinder = $\pi r^2 h \rightarrow 50\pi=\pi r^2 h=\pi(2)^2 h \rightarrow h=12.5$,The height of the cylinder is 12.5 inches which is bigger than 10 inches.

32) Choice A is correct.

Simplify quantity B. Quantity B: $(\frac{x}{6})^6=\frac{x^6}{6^6}$, Since, the two quantities have the same numerator (x^6) and the denominator in quantity B is bigger ($6^6>6$), then the quantity A is greater. (remember that x is an integer)

33) Choice D is correct.

Choose different values for x and find the value of quantity A.$x=1$, then:

Quantity A: $\frac{1}{x}+x=\frac{1}{1}+1=2$,

Quantity B is greater, $x=0.1$, then:

Quantity A: $\frac{1}{x}+x=\frac{1}{0.1}+1=10+1=11$,

Quantity A is greater. The relationship cannot be determined from the information given.

34) Choice D is correct

Simply change the fractions to decimals. $\frac{4}{5}=0.80, \frac{6}{7}=0.857\ldots, \frac{5}{6}=0.8333\ldots$,

As you can see, x lies between 0.80 and 0.857... and it can be 0.81 or 0.84. The first one is less than 0.833... and the second one is greater than 0.833... . The relationship cannot be determined from the information given.

35) Choice C is correct

Choose different values for a and b and find the values of quantity A and quantity B.

$a=2$ and $b=3$, then: Quantity A: $|2-3|=|-1|=1$, Quantity B: $|3-2|=|1|=1$

The two quantities are equal. $a=-3$ and $b=2$, then:

Quantity A: $|-3-2|=|-5|=5$, Quantity B: $|2-(-3)|=|2+3|=5$

The two quantities are equal. Any other values of a and b give the same answer.

36) Choice A is correct

$2x^3+10=64 \rightarrow 2x^3=64-10=54 \rightarrow x^3=\frac{54}{2}=27 \rightarrow x=\sqrt[3]{27}=\sqrt[3]{3^3}=3$

$120 - 18y = 84 \rightarrow -18y = 84 - 120 = -36 \rightarrow y = \frac{-36}{-18} = 2$

37) Choice C is correct.

Quantity A is: $\frac{3+4+x}{3} = 3 \rightarrow x = 2$, Quantity B is: $\frac{2+(2-6)+(2+4)+(2\times2)}{4} = 2$

ISEE Middle LEVEL Math Practice Test 1 Section 2

1) Choice C is correct

50% of 46 is: $\frac{50}{100} \times 46 = \frac{46}{2} = 23$, Let x be the number then: $x = 23 - 5 = 18$

2) Choice C is correct

$4 \times \left(\frac{1}{3} - \frac{1}{6}\right) + 5 = 4 \times \left(\frac{2-1}{6}\right) + 5 = \frac{4}{6} + 5 = \frac{2}{3} + 5 = \frac{17}{3} = 5.6 \ldots$

3) Choice A is correct

20% of $120 = \frac{20}{100} \times 120 = 24$, Let x be the number, then, $x = 24 + 15 = 39$

4) Choice D is correct

Number of pencils are blue$= 85 - 42 = 43$, Percent of blue pencils is: $\frac{43}{85} \times 100 = 50.58\% \cong 51\%$

5) Choice D is correct

$(x+6)^3 = 64 \rightarrow x + 6 = \sqrt[3]{64} = \sqrt[3]{4^3} = 4 \rightarrow x = 4 - 6 = -2$

6) Choice B is correct

The ratio of red to blue balls is 3: 2. Then: $\frac{3}{2} = \frac{x}{90} \rightarrow x = \frac{90\times3}{2} = 135$

7) Choice C is correct

The perimeter of rectangle is: $2 \times (5 + 8) = 2 \times 13 = 26$

The perimeter of circle is: $2\pi r = 2 \times 3 \times \frac{12}{2} = 36$, Difference in perimeter is: $36 - 26 = 10$

8) Choice C is correct

Let x be the number. Write the equation and solve for x. $(27 - x) \div x = 2$, Multiply both sides by x. $(28 - x) = 2x$, then add x both sides. $27 = 3x$, now divide both sides by 3. $x = 9$

9) Choice A is correct

If $\frac{3x}{2} = 15$, then $3x = 30 \rightarrow x = 10$, $\frac{2x}{5} = \frac{2\times10}{5} = \frac{20}{5} = 4$

10) Choice B is correct

Use this formula: Percent of Change $= \frac{New\ Value - Old\ Value}{Old\ Value} \times 100\%$

$\frac{15,000-20,000}{20,000} \times 100\% = -25\%$ and $\frac{11,200-15,000}{15,000} \times 100\% = -25\%$ (negative signs means the price decreased)

11) Choice C is correct

$\frac{1}{4} = 0.25 \qquad \frac{7}{9} = 0.77 \qquad 75\% = 0.75$

0.85 is the greatest number provided.

12) Choice D is correct

$Area = \pi r^2 = \pi \times (\frac{10}{2})^2 = 25\pi = 25 \times 3.14 = 78.5$

13) Choice C is correct

Only choice C is equal to 90.

$\left(\left(\frac{3}{2} + 3\right) \times \frac{18}{3}\right) + 63 = \left(\left(\frac{3+6}{2}\right) \times \frac{18}{3}\right) + 63 = \left(\frac{9}{2} \times \frac{18}{3}\right) + 63 = 27 + 63 = 90$

14) Choice A is correct

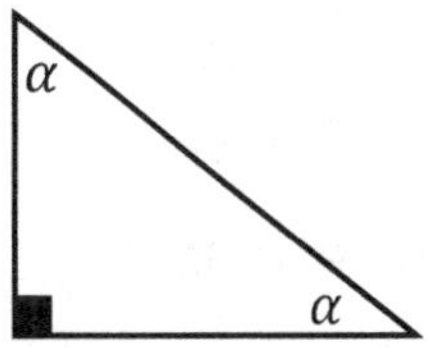

All angles in a triangle sum up to 180 degrees. Then:

$2\alpha + 90° = 180° \rightarrow 2\alpha = 90 \rightarrow \alpha = 45°$

15) Choice B is correct

First, find the number. Let x be the number. Write the equation and solve for x.

120% of a number is 84, then: $1.2 \times x = 84 \Rightarrow x = 84 \div 1.2 = 70$

90% of 70 is: $0.9 \times 70 = 63$

16) Choice D is correct

Find the difference of each pairs of numbers: 3, 4, 6, 9, 13, 18, 24, ___, 39

The difference of 3 and 4 is 1, 4 and 6 is 2, 6 and 9 is 3, 9 and 13 is 4, 13 and 18 is 5, 18 and 24 is 6, 24 and next number should be 7. The number is $24 + 7 = 31$

17) Choice B is correct

The sum of angles in rectangle is 360°

18) Choice A is correct

Let x be the number of shoes the team can purchase. Therefore, the team can purchase $130x$.

The team had \$25,000 and spent \$15,000. Now the team can spend on new shoes \$10,000 at most. Now, write the inequality: $130x + 15,000 \leq 25,000$

19) Choice C is correct

The capacity of a red box is 30% greater than a blue box. Let x be the capacity of the blue box. Then: $x + 30\%\ of\ x = 52 \rightarrow 1.3x = 52 \rightarrow x = \frac{52}{1.3} = 40$

20) Choice B is correct

$\frac{1.75}{1.40} = 1.25 = 125\%$

21) Choice C is correct

$\frac{2}{3} \times 30 = \frac{60}{3} = 20$

22) Choice B is correct

$60\ minutes\ = 1\ Hours \rightarrow \frac{190}{60} = 3.16\ Hours$

23) Choice D is correct

58 is not prime number, it is divisible by 2 and 29.

24) Choice C is correct

The area of the square is 36 inches. Therefore, the side of the square is square root of the area. $\sqrt{36} = 6$ inches, four times the side of the square is the perimeter: $4 \times 6 = 24$ inches

25) Choice D is correct

$13 is what percent of $26? $13 \div 26 = 0.50 = 50\%$

26) Choice D is correct

$\$1.80 \div 36 = \$0.05$

27) Choice A is correct

Let x be one-kilogram orange cost, then: $2x + (2 \times 4.2) = 26.4 \rightarrow 2x + 8.4 = 26.4 \rightarrow$ $2x = 26.4 - 8.4 \rightarrow 2x = 18 \rightarrow x = \frac{18}{2} = \$9$

28) Choice D is correct

Use PEMDAS (order of operation):

$[6 \times (-24) + 8] - (-4) + [6 \times 5] \div 2\ = [-144\ +\ 8] - (-4) +\ [30] \div\ 2$
$= \ [-144\ +\ 8] - (-4) + 15\ =$

$[-136] - (-4) + 15\ = [-136] + 4 + 15\ = -117$

29) Choice B is correct

The width of a rectangle is $3x$ and its length is $5x$. Therefore, the perimeter of the rectangle is $16x$. $Perimeter\ of\ a\ rectangle = 2(width + length) = 2(3x + 5x) = 2(8x) = 16x$

The perimeter of the rectangle is 80. Then: $16x = 80 \rightarrow x = 5$

30) Choice D is correct

The distance between Jason and Joe is 15 miles. Jason running at 5.5 miles per hour and Joe is running at the speed of 7 miles per hour. Therefore, every hour the distance is 1.5 miles less. $15 \div 1.5 = 10$

31) Choice D is correct

$\left(((-12)+20)\times 3\right)+(-16)=((8)\times 3)-16=24-16=8$

32) Choice A is correct

The percent of girls playing tennis is: $45\% \times 20\% = 0.45 \times 0.20 = 0.09 = 9\%$

33) Choice D is correct

Let x be the original price. If the price of the sofa is decreased by 30% to $\$490$, then: $70\%\ of\ x = 490 \Rightarrow 0.70x = 490 \Rightarrow x = 490 \div 0.70 = 700$

34) Choice A is correct

There are twice as many girls as boys. Let x be the number of girls in the class. Then:

$x + 2x = 45 \rightarrow 3x = 45 \rightarrow x = 15$

35) Choice C is correct

The ratio of lions to tigers is 5 to 3 at the zoo. Therefore, total number of lions and tigers must be divisible by 8. $5 + 3 = 8$, From the numbers provided, only 97 is not divisible by 8.

36) Choice A is correct

$10x = -55.5 + 15.5 = -40 \rightarrow x = \frac{-40}{10} = -4$

37) Choice A is correct

0.25 minutes equals 15 seconds. Then, the number of rotates in 15 second$= \frac{400\times15}{5} = 1{,}200$

38) Choice A is correct

Use formula of rectangle prism volume. $V = (length)(width)(height) \Rightarrow$

$$2{,}500 = (40)\ (10)\ (height) \Rightarrow height = 2{,}500 \div 400 = 6.25$$

39) Choice C is correct

$$7{,}776 = 6^5 \rightarrow 6^x = 6^5 \rightarrow x = 5$$

40) Choice B is correct

$10 + 5(x + 5 - 5x) = 10 + 5(-4x + 5) = 40 \rightarrow 10 - 20x + 25 = 40 \rightarrow -20x + 35 = 40$

$$\rightarrow -20x = 5 \rightarrow x = -\frac{1}{4}$$

41) Choice B is correct

The area of trapezoid is: $\left(\frac{8+10}{2}\right) \times 5 = 45$

42) Choice D is correct

$$13.125 \div 0.005 = \frac{\frac{13{,}125}{1{,}000}}{\frac{5}{1{,}000}} = \frac{13{,}125}{5} = 2{,}625$$

43) Choice B is correct

The probability of choosing a Hearts is $\frac{13}{52} = \frac{1}{4}$

44) Choice B is correct

$20 - 13.59 = \$6.41$

45) Choice C is correct

$$\frac{5 \times 20}{80} = \frac{100}{80} = 1.25 \cong 1.3$$

46) Choice C is correct

Write the equation and solve for B: $0.60A = 0.30B$, divide both sides by 0.30, then you will have $\frac{0.60}{0.30}A = B$, therefore: $B = 2A$, and B is 2 times of A or it's 200% of A.

47) Choice C is correct

$$\frac{3}{4} + \frac{\frac{-3}{5}}{\frac{6}{10}} = \frac{3}{4} + \frac{(-3) \times 10}{5 \times 6} = \frac{3}{4} + \frac{-30}{30} = \frac{3}{4} - 1 = \frac{3-4}{4} = -\frac{1}{4}$$

ISEE Middle LEVEL Math Practice Test 2 Section 1

1) Choice A is correct

$343 = 7^3 \rightarrow \frac{7^x}{7} = 7^3 \rightarrow 7^{x-1} = 7^3 \rightarrow x - 1 = 3 \rightarrow x = 4$

2) Choice B is correct

In triangle sum of all angles equal to $180°$ then: $y = 180° - (120° + 30°) = 180° - 150° = 30°$

3) Choice B is correct

$\frac{1}{3} \cong 0.33$ $\quad \frac{4}{7} \cong 0.57$ $\quad \frac{8}{12} \cong 0.66$ $\quad \frac{3}{4} = 0.75$

4) Choice C is correct

One hour equal to 60 minutes then, $5\ hours = 5 \times 60 = 300\ minutes$

One minute equal to 60 seconds then, $300\ minutes = 300 \times 60 = 18{,}000\ seconds$

Distance that travel by object is: $0.4 \times 18{,}000 = 7{,}200\ cm = 72\ m$

5) Choice B is correct

Number of visiting fans: $\frac{2\times24{,}000}{5} = 9{,}600$

6) Choice A is correct

Circumference of circle= $2\pi r = 2\pi \times \frac{17}{2} = 17\pi \sim 53.38\,m$

7) Choice B is correct

The lowest common multiple of 24 and 36 is 72.

8) Choice A is correct

Area of circle with diameter 8 is: $\pi r^2 = \pi\left(\frac{8}{2}\right)^2 = 16\pi,$ The area of shaded region is: $\frac{16\pi}{4} = 4\pi$

9) Choice D is correct

30% of $200 = \frac{30}{100} \times 200 = 60,$ Final sale price is: $200 - 60 = \$140$

10) Choice D is correct

To find the discount, multiply the number by $(100\% - rate\ of\ discount)$.

Therefore, for the first discount we get: $(300)\ (100\% - 15\%) = (300)\ (0.85)$

For the next 25% discount: $(300)\ (0.85)\ (0.75)$

11) Choice C is correct

The amount of petrol consumed after x hours is: $5x$, Petrol remaining: $70 - 5x$

12) Choice A is correct

$4 + x + 8\left(\frac{x}{4}\right) = 2x + 12 \rightarrow 4 + x + 2x = 2x + 12 \rightarrow x = 8$

13) Choice B is correct

The area of trapezoid is: $\left(\frac{16+18}{2}\right)x = 136 \rightarrow 17x = 136 \rightarrow x = 8$

14) Choice A is correct

$\frac{3}{5}$ of $280 = \frac{3}{5} \times 280 = 168$, $\frac{1}{2}$ of $168 = \frac{1}{2} \times 168 = 84$, $\frac{1}{3}$ of $84 = \frac{1}{3} \times 84 = 28$

15) Choice B is correct

$6 + 3x \leq 21 \rightarrow 3x \leq 21 - 6 \rightarrow 3x \leq 15 \rightarrow x \leq \frac{15}{3} \rightarrow x \leq 5,$ Then: $a = 5$

16) Choice B is correct

$One\ liter = 1{,}000\ cm^3 \rightarrow 7\ liters = 7{,}000\ cm^3$, $7{,}000 = 25 \times 5 \times h \rightarrow h = \frac{7{,}000}{125} = 56\ cm$

17) Choice C is correct

$4f + 4g = 4x - 2y \rightarrow 4f + 4(2y - 6x) = 4x - 2y \rightarrow 4f + 8y - 24x = 4x - 2y \rightarrow$

$4f = 28x - 10y \rightarrow 2f = 14x - 5y$

18) Choice A is correct

$$\frac{-\frac{13}{3}\times\frac{4}{5}}{\frac{10}{30}} = -\frac{\frac{13\times4}{3\times5}}{\frac{10}{30}} = -\frac{\frac{52}{15}}{\frac{10}{30}} = -\frac{52\times30}{15\times10} = -10.4$$

19) Choice A is correct

Use Pythagorean theorem to find the value of c: $a^2 + b^2 = c^2 \rightarrow 5^2 + 12^2 = c^2 \rightarrow$

$169 = c^2 \rightarrow \text{c} = 13$. Perimeter of parallelogram$= (9 + 5 + 13) \times 2 = 54$

20) Choice C is correct

$$\frac{6}{50} \times 100 = \frac{6}{5} \times 10 = 12\%$$

21) Choice A is correct

Let x be the integer. Then: $2x - 3 = 71$, Add 3 both sides: $2x = 74$, Divide both sides by 2: $x = 37$

22) Choice D is correct

$$\frac{0.35}{8.5} \times 100 = 4.11 \approx 4.00$$

23) Choice D is correct

Plug in 140 for F and then solve for C. $C = \frac{5}{9}(F - 32) \Rightarrow C = \frac{5}{9}(140 - 32) \Rightarrow$

$$C = \frac{5}{9}(108) = 60$$

24) Choice D is correct

$$Average = \frac{sum\ of\ terms}{number\ of\ terms} \Rightarrow 20 = \frac{14+16+21+x}{4} \Rightarrow 80 = 51 + x \Rightarrow x = 29$$

25) Choice B is correct

First write the numbers in the order: 2,2,2,3,3,4,4,5,5,6,6

The mode of numbers is: 2 median is: 4

26) Choice A is correct.

Column A: Simplify. $\frac{\sqrt{64-48}}{\sqrt{25-9}} = \frac{\sqrt{16}}{\sqrt{16}} = 1$

Column B: $\frac{(7-4)}{(8-3)} = \frac{3}{5}$

27) Choice B is correct

$2x^5 - 9 = 477 \rightarrow 2x^5 = 477 + 9 = 486 \rightarrow x^5 = \frac{486}{2} = 243 \rightarrow x = \sqrt[5]{243} = \sqrt[5]{3^5} = 3$

$\frac{1}{3} - \frac{y}{5} = -\frac{7}{15} \rightarrow \frac{y}{5} = \frac{1}{3} + \frac{7}{15} = \frac{5+7}{15} = \frac{12}{15} = \frac{4}{5} \rightarrow y = 5 \times \frac{4}{5} = 4$

28) Choice A is correct.

Column A: First, find the integers. Let x be the smallest integer. Then the integers are x, $(x+1)$, and $(x+2)$. The sum of the integers is -45. Then:

$x + x + 1 + x + 2 = -45 \rightarrow 3x + 3 = -45 \rightarrow 3x = -48 \rightarrow x = -16$

The smallest integer is -16, therefore, the largest integer is bigger than that.

29) Choice C is correct.

Column A: $4^2 - 2^4 = 16 - 16 = 0$

Column B: $2^4 - 4^2 = 16 - 16 = 0$

30) Choice C is correct.

Column A: 8% of the computer cost is 20: $8\% \times 250 = 0.08 \times 250 = 20$

Column B: 20

31) Choice C is correct.

Column A: The slope of the line $4x + 2y = 7$ is -2.

Write the equation in slope intercept form. $4x + 2y = 7 \rightarrow 2y = -4x + 7 \rightarrow y = -2x + \frac{7}{2}$

Column B: The slope of the line that passes through points $(2, 5)$ and $(3, 3)$:

Use slope formula: $slope\ of\ a\ line = \frac{y_2 - y_1}{x_2 - x_1} = \frac{3-5}{3-2} = -2$

32) Choice A is correct

prime factoring of 55 is: 5×11 , prime factoring of 210 is: $2 \times 3 \times 5 \times 7$

Quantity $A = 5$ and Quantity $B = 2$

33) Choice A is correct.

Column A: Simplify. $\sqrt{144 - 81} = \sqrt{63}$

Column B: $\sqrt{144} - \sqrt{81} = 12 - 9 = 3$

$\sqrt{63}$ is bigger than 3. ($\sqrt{9} = 3$)

34) Choice B is correct

6% of x = 5% of $y \rightarrow 0.06\,x = 0.05\,y \rightarrow x = \frac{0.05}{0.06} y \rightarrow x = \frac{5}{6} y$, therefore, y is bigger than x.

35) Choice C is correct

Simplify both quantities.

Quantity A: $(-5)^4 = (-5) \times (-5) \times (-5) \times (-5) = 625$

Quantity B: $5 \times 5 \times 5 \times 5 = 625$
The two quantities are equal.

36) Choice C is correct.

Use exponent "product rule": $x^n \times x^m = x^{n+m}$

Quantity A: $(1.88)^4(1.88)^8 = (1.88)^{4+8} = (1.88)^{12}$

Quantity B: $(1.88)^{12}$
The two quantities are equal.

37) Choice D is correct.

Choose different values for x and find the value of quantity A and quantity B.

$x = 1$, then: Quantity A: $x^{10} = 1^{10} = 1$

Quantity B: $x^{20} = 1^{20} = 1$

The two quantities are equal.

$x = 2$, then: Quantity A: $x^{10} = 2^{10}$

Quantity B: $x^{20} = 2^{20}$

Quantity B is greater.

Therefore, the relationship cannot be determined from the information given

ISEE Middle LEVEL Math Practice Test 2 Section 2

1) Choice A is correct

20 cubed is: $20^3 = 8{,}000$

2) Choice A is correct

$3^x + 28 = 55 \rightarrow 3^x = 55 - 28 = 27$ and $27 = 3^3, 3^x = 3^3 \rightarrow x = 3$

3) Choice D is correct
All angles in a parallelogram sum up to 360 degrees. Since, we only have 2 angles, therefore the answer cannot be determined.
4) Choice D is correct

Prime factorizing of $10 = 2 \times 5$, Prime factorizing of $35 = 5 \times 7$

$x = LCM = 2 \times 5 \times 7 = 70$, $\frac{70}{5} + 2 = 14 + 2 = 16$

5) Choice B is correct

The area of trapezoid is: $\left(\frac{8+12}{2}\right) \times x = 30 \rightarrow 10x = 30 \rightarrow x = 3$

$y = \sqrt{3^2 + 4^2} = 5$, Perimeter is: $12 + 3 + 8 + 5 = 28$

6) Choice B is correct

Swing moves once from point A to point B and returns to point A is: $20 + 20 = 40$ seconds

Therefore, for ten times: $5 \times 40 = 200$ seconds

7) Choice D is correct

Speed of the blue car: $1\frac{2}{5} \times 40 = 56$, Difference of the cars' speed: $56 - 40 = 16$, The red car is $12\ km$ ahead of a blue car. Therefore, it takes the blue car 45 minutes to catch the red car.
$\frac{12}{16} = \frac{3}{3}$ Hour $= 45$ minutes

8) Choice D is correct

The population is increased by 10% and 25%. 10% increase changes the population to 110% of original population. For the second increase, multiply the result by 125%.

$(1.10) \times (1.25) = 1.37 = 137\%$, 37 percent of the population is increased after two years.

9) Choice C is correct

Use PEMDAS (order of operation): $5 + 8 \times (-2) - [4 + 22 \times 5] \div 6 = 5 + 8 \times (-2) - [4 + 110] \div 6 = 5 + 8 \times (-2) - [114] \div 6 = 5 + (-16) - 19 = 5 + (-16) - 19 = -11 - 19 = -30$

10) Choice A is correct

Let x be the number of years. Therefore, \$2,500 per year equals $2{,}500x$. starting from \$26,000 annual salary means you should add that amount to $2{,}500x$. Income more than that is: $I > 2{,}500\,x + 26{,}000$

11) Choice D is correct

Angle between 90° and 180° is called obtuse angle.

12) Choice A is correct

2,500 out of 65,000 equals to $\frac{2{,}500}{65{,}000} = \frac{25}{650} = \frac{1}{26}$

13) Choice B is correct

$$Probability = \frac{number\ of\ desired\ outcomes}{\text{number of total outcomes}} = \frac{19}{13+19+19+25} = \frac{19}{76} = \frac{1}{4}$$

14) Choice D is correct

Only choice D equals 110: $(2 \times 10) + (50 \times 1.5) + 15 = 20 + 75 + 15 = 110$

15) Choice D is correct

The area of rectangle is: $8 \times 4 = 32\ cm^2$, The area of circle is: $\pi r^2 = \pi \times (\frac{8}{2})^2 = 3 \times 16 = 48$, Difference in area is: $48 - 32 = 16$

16) Choice B is correct

$x^2 + 2x + 1 = (x + 1)^2 \rightarrow (x + 1)^2 = 64 \rightarrow x + 1 = 8 \rightarrow x = 7 \text{ or } x + 1 = -8 \rightarrow x = -9$

17) Choice C is correct

Perimeter $A = 4 \times 6 = 24,$ Area $B = 2 \times 4 = 8,\ \frac{24}{8} = 3$

18) Choice A is correct

$\frac{18 \times 21}{5} = \frac{378}{5} = 75.6$

19) Choice B is correct

To find the number of possible outfit combinations, multiply number of options for each factor: $4 \times 2 \times 5 = 40$

20) Choice A is correct

Let x be the number, then: $x^2 + 9 = 25 \rightarrow x^2 = 16 \rightarrow x^2 - 16 = 0 \rightarrow (x + 4)(x - 4) = 0 \rightarrow x = 4 \text{ or } x = -4$

21) Choice D is correct

8% of \$2,000 = $\frac{8}{100} \times 2{,}000 = \$160$

22) Choice A is correct

$\frac{x}{4} + \frac{5}{4} = \frac{30}{6} \rightarrow \frac{x}{4} = 5 - \frac{5}{4} = \frac{20 - 5}{4} = \frac{15}{4} = \frac{x}{4} \rightarrow x = 4 \times \frac{15}{4} = 15$

23) Choice D is correct

$y = 5ab\ + 3b^3$, Plug in the values of a and b in the equation: $a = 3$ and $b = 2$

$y = 5\,(3)(2) + 3\,(2)^3 = 30 + 3(8) = 30 + 24 = 54$

24) Choice D is correct

$|6 - 10| = |-4| = 4$

25) Choice C is correct

The angles of an equilateral triangle are 60, 60, 60 degrees.

26) Choice C is correct

$9x - 10 = 5\left(\frac{4}{5}x - y\right) + 5 \rightarrow 9x - 10 = 4x - 5y + 5 \rightarrow 5x - 10 = -5y + 5$

$\rightarrow 5x = -5y + 15 \rightarrow x = -y + 3 \rightarrow x + y = 3$

27) Choice C is correct

The area of the floor is: $7cm\ \times\ 27\ cm = 189\ cm^2$, The number is tiles needed $= 189 \div 3 = 63$

28) Choice B is correct

Let x be price of one-kilogram of apple and y be price of one-kilogram of orange, then:

$x = 2y,\ 2x + 3y = 21 \rightarrow 2(2y) + 3y = 21 \rightarrow 7y = 21 \rightarrow y = \frac{21}{7} = 3 \rightarrow x = 2 \times 3 = 6$

29) Choice D is correct

122 is not prime number, it is divided by 2

30) Choice D is correct

Since, each of the x students in a team may invite up to 6 friends, the maximum number of people in the party is 7 times x or $7x$. $(one\ student + 6\ friends = 7\ people)$

31) Choice C is correct

Perimeter= $2\pi r = 2 \times \pi \times \frac{10}{2} = 10 \approx 31.4 \approx 31$

32) Choice B is correct

$60\ minutes = 1\ Hour \rightarrow \frac{280}{60} = 4.6\ Hours$

33) Choice A is correct

Let x be the weight of the red box. Then: Weight of blue box: $0.8x = 60 \rightarrow x = \frac{60}{0.8} = 75,$

Weight of yellow box $1.20y = 75 \rightarrow y = 62.5$

The weight of all boxes: $60 + 75 + 62.5 = 197.5$

34) Choice D is correct

$180° - 40° = 140°$

35) Choice B is correct

Average speed: $\frac{350}{9} = 38.8\ miles\ per\ hour$

36) Choice B is correct

Let x be the price that third person has to pay then; $58 = 7.5 + (2 \times 7.5) + x \rightarrow$

$x = 58 - 22.5 = 35.5$

37) Choice D is correct

$$\left(\left((-15) + 40\right) \times \frac{1}{5}\right) + (-15) = \left((25) \times \frac{1}{5}\right) - 15 = 5 - 15 = -10$$

38) Choice D is correct

$138{,}210 = 1.3821 \times 10^5$

39) Choice B is correct

$(10 - 6)! = 4! = 4 \times 3 \times 2 \times 1 = 24$

40) Choice D is correct

$c = \sqrt{4^2 + 3^2} = \sqrt{25} = 5$, Perimeter is: $5 + 3 + 4 = 12$

41) Choice A is correct

Let x be the number then, 150% of $x = 1.5x$, $1.5x = 0.30 \times 80 = 24 \rightarrow x = \frac{24}{1.5} = 16$

42) Choice A is correct

Number of employees with Diploma: $\frac{4 \times 24}{1} = 96$

That means there are 24 employees with Bachelor's Degree and 96 employees with high school diploma. To get the ratio of employees with Bachelor's Degree to the number of employees with High School Diploma 3 to 4, there should be 32 employees with high school diploma. So, 40 $(96 - 32 = 64)$ employees with High School Diploma should be moved to other departments.

43) Choice B is correct

Use Pythagorean theorem: $x^2 + 20^2 = 25^2 \rightarrow x^2 = 25^2 - 20^2 \rightarrow x = \sqrt{25^2 - 20^2} \rightarrow x = \sqrt{625 - 400} = \sqrt{225} = 15$

44) Choice D is correct

$average = \frac{sum\ of\ terms}{number\ of\ terms}$, The sum of the weight of all girls is: $20 \times 65 = 1{,}300\ kg$

The sum of the weight of all boys is: $35 \times 72 = 2{,}520\ kg$, The sum of the weight of all students is: $1{,}300 + 2{,}520 = 3{,}820\ kg$, $Average = \frac{3{,}820}{55} = 69.45$

45) Choice A is correct

The sum of supplement angles is 180. Let x be that angle. Therefore, $x + 9x = 180$, $10x = 180$, divide both sides by 10: $x = 18$

46) Choice D is correct

Smallest 5–digit number is 10,000, and biggest 5–digit number is 99,999. The difference is: 89,999 ,

47) Choice A is correct

The average speed of john is: $140 \div 5 = 28$, The average speed of Alice is: $210 \div 3 = 70$

Write the ratio and simplify. $28 : 70 \Rightarrow 2 : 5$

ISEE Middle Level Practice Test 3 Section 1

1) Choice C is correct

$\frac{1}{5} \cong 0.2$ $\quad \frac{3}{8} \cong 0.37$ $\quad \frac{2}{5} = 0.4$ $\quad \frac{5}{4} = 1.25$

2) Choice B is correct

$542{,}357{,}841 \times \frac{1}{10{,}000} = 54{,}235.7841$

3) Choice C is correct

16% off equals $40. Let x be the original price of the table. Then:

$16\%\ of\ x = 40 \rightarrow 0.16x = 40 \rightarrow x = \frac{40}{0.16} = 250$

4) Choice B is correct

Use the formula for Percent of Change: $\frac{\text{New Value} - \text{Old Value}}{Old\ Value} \times 100\%$

$\frac{27-42}{42} \times 100\% = -35\%$ (negative sign here means that the new price is less than old price)

5) Choice C is correct

$4f = 4 \times (2x - 3y) = 8x - 12y,\ \ 4f + g = 8x - 12y + x + 7y = 9x - 5y$

6) Choice B is correct

$\frac{-48 \times 0.5}{6} = -\frac{48 \times \frac{1}{2}}{6} = -\frac{\frac{48}{2}}{6} = -\frac{48}{12} = -4$

7) Choice C is correct

$8^x = 512, , 8^3 = 512 \rightarrow x = 3$ Choice C is correct.

8) Choice A is correct

If the score of Mia was 80, therefore the score of Ava is 40. Since, the score of Emma was half as that of Ava, therefore, the score of Emma is 20.

9) Choice B is correct

Use the formula of areas of circles. $Area\ of\ a\ circle = \pi r^2 \Rightarrow 81\,\pi = \pi r^2 \Rightarrow 81 = r^2 \Rightarrow r = 9$, Radius of the circle is 9. Now, use the circumference formula: Circumference $= 2\pi r = 2\pi\,(9) = 18\,\pi$

10) Choice D is correct

$1.16 = \frac{116}{100}$ and $7.4 = \frac{74}{10}$ $\rightarrow 1.16 \times 7.4 = \frac{116}{100} \times \frac{74}{10} = \frac{8{,}584}{1{,}000} = 8.584 \cong 8.6$

11) Choice D is correct

Supplementary angles sum up to 180 degrees. x and 55 degrees are supplementary angles. Then: $x = 180° - 55° = 125°$

12) Choice D is correct

Let x be the number. Write the equation and solve for x. $\frac{2}{3} \times 9 = \frac{2}{7} \times x \Rightarrow \frac{2\times9}{3} = \frac{2x}{7}$, use cross multiplication to solve for x. $7 \times 18 = 2x \times 3 \Rightarrow 126 = 6x \Rightarrow x = 21$

13) Choice C is correct

The square root of 169 is 13 which is closest to the square root of 170.

14) Choice D is correct

Use rectangle prism volume formula: $V = w \times l \times h \rightarrow 960 = w \times 8 \times 12 \rightarrow w = \frac{960}{96} = 10$

15) Choice D is correct

The perimeter of the trapezoid is 58.

Therefore, the missing side (height) is $= 58 - 10 - 12 - 15 = 21$

Area of the trapezoid: $A = \frac{1}{2} h (b_1 + b_2) = \frac{1}{2} (21)(12 + 10) = 231$

16) Choice D is correct

Let x be the original price. If the price of a laptop is decreased by 60% to $\$460$, then:

40% of $x = 460 \Rightarrow 0.40x = 460 \Rightarrow x = 460 \div 0.40 = 1{,}150$

17) Choice B is correct

$\frac{1}{3}$ of $120 = \frac{1}{3} \times 120 = 40$, $\frac{1}{5}$ of $40 = \frac{1}{5} \times 40 = 8$

18) Choice C is correct

The ratio of boy to girls is $3:8$. Therefore, there are 3 boys out of 11 students. To find the answer, first divide the total number of students by 11, then multiply the result by 3.

$55 \div 11 = 5 \Rightarrow 5 \times 3 = 15$,There are 15 boys and 40 $(55 - 15)$ girls. So, 25 more boys should be enrolled to make the ratio $1:1$

19) Choice B is correct

Simplify: $4(x + 1) = 6(x + 4) - 28$, $4x + 4 = 6x + 24 - 28$, $4x + 4 = 6x - 4$

Subtract $4x$ from both sides: $4 = 2x - 4$, Add 4 to both sides: $8 = 2x, 4 = x$

20) Choice C is correct

Let x be the sales profit. Then, 4% of sales profit is $0.04x$. Employee's revenue: $0.04x + 8{,}000$

21) Choice D is correct

Let's review the choices:

A. $\frac{3}{4} > 0.9$ This is not a correct statement. Because $\frac{3}{4} = 0.75$ and it's less than 0.9.
B. $11\% = \frac{2}{5}$ This is not a correct statement. Because $11\% = 0.11$ and $\frac{2}{5} = 0.4$
C. $3.5 < \frac{7}{3}$ This is not a correct statement. Because $\frac{7}{3} = 2.33$ and it's less than 3.5.
D. $\frac{6}{7} > 0.8$ This is a correct statement. $\frac{6}{7} = 0.85 \rightarrow 0.8 < \frac{6}{7}$

22) Choice B is correct

$x = 35 + 115 = 150$

23) Choice B is correct

The diagonal of the square is 4. Let x be the side. Use Pythagorean Theorem: $a^2 + b^2 = c^2$

$x^2 + x^2 = 4^2 \Rightarrow 2x^2 = 4^2 \Rightarrow 2x^2 = 16 \Rightarrow x^2 = 8 \Rightarrow x = \sqrt{8}$. The area of the square is: $\sqrt{8} \times \sqrt{8} = 8$

24) Choice A is correct

$-28 - (-75) = -28 + 75 = 75 - 28 = 47$

25) Choice A is correct

Petrol of car A in $150\ km = \frac{6\times150}{100} = 9$, Petrol of car B in $150\ km = \frac{4\times150}{100} = 6, 9 - 6 = 3$

26) Choice C is correct.

Column A: Simplify. $\sqrt{25} + \sqrt{25} = 5 + 5 = 10$, 10 is equal to $\sqrt{100}$ ($\sqrt{100} = 10$)

27) Choice D is correct.

Based on information provided, we cannot find the average age of Joe and Michelle or average age of Michelle and Nicole.

28) Choice A is correct.

Column A: Use order of operation to calculate the result. $5 + 5 \times 7 - 4 = 5 + 35 - 4 = 36$

Column B: $4 + 6 \times 6 - 6 \rightarrow 4 + 36 - 6 = 34$

29) Choice A is correct.

Column A: The value of x when $y = 9 : y = 3x + 18 \rightarrow 9 = 3x + 18 \rightarrow 3x = -9 \rightarrow x = -3$

Column B: -4, -3 is greater than -4.

30) Choice A is correct.

Column A: Simplify. $\sqrt{144 - 121} = \sqrt{23}$

Column B: $\sqrt{144} - \sqrt{121} = 12 - 11 = 1$, $\sqrt{23}$ is bigger than 1.

31) Choice A is correct

Volume of a right cylinder = $\pi r^2 h \rightarrow 80\pi = \pi r^2 h = \pi(5)^2 h \rightarrow h = 3.2$
The height of the cylinder is 3.2 inches which is bigger than 3 inches.

32) Choice D is correct.

Choose different values for x and find the value of quantity A.

$x = 1$, then: Quantity A: $\frac{2}{x} + x = \frac{2}{1} + 1 = 3$, Quantity B is greater

$x = 0.1$, then: Quantity A: $\frac{2}{x} + x = \frac{2}{0.1} + 1 = 20 + 1 = 21$, Quantity A is greater

The relationship cannot be determined from the information given.

33) Choice B is correct.

Simply change the fractions to decimals. $\frac{2}{5} = 0.40$, $\frac{5}{9} = 0.55 \ldots$, $\frac{5}{8} = 0.625$, Quantity B is greater

34) Choice A is correct.

Simplify quantity B. Quantity B: $(\frac{x}{3})^3 = \frac{x^3}{3^3}$

Since, the two quantities have the same numerator (x^3) and the denominator in quantity B is bigger $(3^3 > 3)$, then the quantity A is greater.

35) Choice A is correct
Quantity A is: $\frac{5+6+x}{3} = 6 \rightarrow x = 7$, Quantity B is: $\frac{7+(7+3)+(7+1)-7}{4} = 4.5$
36) Choice C is correct

Choose different values for a and b and find the values of quantity A and quantity B.

$a = 4$ and $b = 3$, then: Quantity A: $|4 - 3| = |1| = 1$, Quantity B: $|3 - 4| = |1| = 1$

The two quantities are equal. $a = 3$ and $b = -3$, then: Quantity A: $|3 + 3| = |6| = 6$

Quantity B: $|-3 - (3)| = |-6| = 6$, The two quantities are equal.

Any other values of a and b provide the same answer.

37) Choice C is correct

$4x^3 - 80 = 176 \rightarrow 4x^3 = 176 + 80 = 256 \rightarrow x^3 = \frac{256}{4} = 64 \rightarrow x = \sqrt[3]{64} = \sqrt[3]{4^3} = 4$

$3 - 4y = -13 \rightarrow -4y = -13 - 3 = -16 \rightarrow y = \frac{-16}{-4} = 4$

ISEE Middle Level Math Practice Test 3 Section 2

1) Choice B is correct

15% of 120 $= \frac{15}{100} \times 120 = 18$, Let x be the number then, $x = 28 + 18 = 46$

2) Choice B is correct

$\frac{2}{5} \times 60 = 24$

3) Choice B is correct

$3 \times \left(\frac{1}{2} - \frac{1}{8}\right) + 6 = 3 \times \left(\frac{4-1}{8}\right) + 6 = \frac{9}{8} + 6 = \frac{57}{8} = 7.125$

4) Choice D is correct

Number of pencils are blue$= 92 - 45 = 47$, Percent of blue pencils is: $\frac{47}{92} \times 100 = 51.08\% \cong 51\%$

5) Choice B is correct

$(x+9)^3 = 125 \rightarrow x + 9 = \sqrt[3]{125} = \sqrt[3]{5^3} = 5 \rightarrow x = 5 - 9 = -4$

6) Choice B is correct

40% of 36 is: $\frac{40}{100} \times 36 = \frac{1,440}{100} = 14.4$, Let x be the number then: $x = 14.4 - 6 = 8.4$

7) Choice A is correct

The perimeter of rectangle is: $2 \times (4 + 8) = 2 \times 12 = 24$

The perimeter of circle is: $2\pi r = 2 \times 3 \times \frac{18}{2} = 54$, Difference in perimeter is: $54 - 24 = 30$

8) Choice B is correct

$\frac{504}{600} = 0.84$. 504 is 84 percent of 600. So, the discount is 16%. $100\% - 84\% = 16\%$

9) Choice C is correct

Let x be the number. Write the equation and solve for x. $(32 - x) \div x = 3$, Multiply both sides by x. $(32 - x) = 3x$, then add x both sides. $32 = 4x$, now divide both sides by 4. $x = 8$

10) Choice A is correct

Only choice A is correct. $2 + (3 \times 10) + (2 \times 30) = 2 + 30 + 60 = 92$

11) Choice A is correct

If $\frac{2x}{3} = 30$, then $2x = 90 \rightarrow x = 45,\ \frac{2x}{4} = \frac{2\times45}{4} = \frac{90}{4} = 22.5$

12) Choice C is correct

$\frac{1}{2} = 0.5$ $\frac{7}{9} = 0.77$ $55\% = 0.55$

13) Choice B is correct

$Area = \pi r^2 = \pi \times (\frac{30}{2})^2 = 225\pi = 225 \times 3.14 = 706.5$

14) Choice A is correct

First, find the number. Let x be the number. Write the equation and solve for x. 140% of a number is 98, then: $1.4 \times x = 98 \Rightarrow x = 98 \div 1.4 = 70$, 80% of 70 is: $0.8 \times 70 = 56$

15) Choice A is correct

Find the difference of each pairs of numbers: $2, 3, 5, 8, 12, 17,$ ___$, 30$

The difference of 2 and 3 is 1, 3 and 5 is 2, 5 and 8 is 3, 8 and 12 is 4, 12 and 17 is 5, 17 and next number should be 6. The number is $17 + 6 = 23$

16) Choice D is correct

All angles in a triangle sum up to 180 degrees. Only angles in choice D add up to 180 degrees.

17) Choice C is correct

In rectangle sides that face to face each other is equal.

Paper clips cost 48 cents a dozen. It means that each paper clip costs 4 cents: $48 \div 12 = 4$

So, 50 paper clips cost two dollars. $50 \times 4 = 200\ cents = \$2.00$

18) Choice D is correct

$\frac{2}{7} \times 35 = \frac{70}{7} = 10$

19) Choice A is correct

If $A \times A$ is odd then A cannot be zero. A can be prime (for example 3), it can be negative (for example -3), and it should be odd.

20) Choice C is correct

The capacity of a red box is 20% greater than a blue box. Let x be the capacity of the blue box. Then: $x + 20\%\ of\ x = 36 \rightarrow 1.2x = 36 \rightarrow x = \frac{36}{1.2} = 30$

21) Choice C is correct

$\frac{1.85}{1.25} = 1.48 = 148\%$

22) Choice A is correct

$60\ minutes = 1\ hour \rightarrow \frac{198}{60} = 3.3\ hours$

23) Choice D is correct

$\frac{2}{5} \times 45 = \frac{90}{5} = 18$

24) Choice D is correct

69 is not prime number, it is divisible by 3 and 23.

25) Choice C is correct

The area of the square is 49 inches. Therefore, the side of the square is square root of the area. $\sqrt{49} = 7$ inches, four times the side of the square is the perimeter: $4 \times 7 = 28\ inches$

26) Choice D is correct

$14 is what percent of $32? $14 \div 32 = 0.43 = 43\%$

27) Choice B is correct

Let x be one-kilogram orange cost, then: $3x + (2 \times 4.2) = 29.4 \rightarrow 3x + 8.4 = 29.4 \rightarrow$
$3x = 29.4 - 8.4 \rightarrow 3x = 21 \rightarrow x = \frac{21}{3} = \$7$

28) Choice A is correct

$\Big(\big((-14) + 24\big) \times 2\Big) + (-10) = \big((10) \times 2\big) - 10 = 20 - 10 = 10$

29) Choice A is correct

The width of a rectangle is $5x$ and its length is $7x$. Therefore, the perimeter of the rectangle is $24x$. $Perimeter\ of\ a\ rectangle = 2(width + length) = 2(5x + 7x) = 2(12x) = 24x$

The perimeter of the rectangle is 60. Then: $24x = 60 \rightarrow x = 2.5$

30) Choice C is correct

The distance between Jason and Joe is 6 miles. Jason running at 6.5 miles per hour and Joe is running at the speed of 8 miles per hour. Therefore, every hour the distance is 1.5 miles less.

$6 \div 1.5 = 4$

31) Choice D is correct

Use PEMDAS (order of operation):

$$[7\times(-25)+9]-(-2)+[4\times 4]\div 2=[-175+9]-(-2)+[16]\div 2$$
$$=[-175+9]-(-2)+8=[-166]-(-2)+8=[-166]+2+8=-156$$

32) Choice A is correct

The percent of girls playing tennis is: $35\% \times 24\% = 0.35 \times 0.24 = 0.08 = 8\%$

33) Choice A is correct

There are twice as many girls as boys. Let x be the number of girls in the class. Then:

$x + 2x = 57 \rightarrow 3x = 57 \rightarrow x = 19$

34) Choice C is correct

The ratio of lions to tigers is 5 to 1 at the zoo. Therefore, total number of lions and tigers must be divisible by 6. $5 + 1 = 6$. From the numbers provided, only 79 is not divisible by 6.

35) Choice C is correct

Let x be the original price. If the price of the sofa is decreased by 20% to \$560, then: $80\%\ of\ x = 560 \Rightarrow 0.80x = 560 \Rightarrow x = 560 \div 0.80 = 700$

36) Choice A is correct

Number of rotates in 14 second= $\frac{100\times 14}{3.5} = 400$

37) Choice A is correct

$10x = -46.5 + 16.5 = -30 \rightarrow x = \frac{-30}{10} = -3$

38) Choice D is correct

Use formula of rectangle prism volume.

$$V = (length)\ (width)\ (height) \Rightarrow 3{,}000 = (50)\ (6)\ (height) \Rightarrow height = 3{,}000 \div 300 = 10$$

39) Choice B is correct

$216 = 6^3 \quad \rightarrow 6^x = 6^3 \rightarrow x = 3$

40) Choice B is correct

The area of trapezoid is: $\left(\frac{12+14}{2}\right) \times 5 = 65$

41) Choice D is correct

$$14.124 \div 0.005 = \frac{\frac{14{,}124}{1{,}000}}{\frac{5}{1{,}000}} = \frac{14{,}124}{5} = 2{,}824.8$$

42) Choice A is correct

$$10 + 6(x + 2 - 2x) = 10 + 6(-x + 2) = 28 \rightarrow 10 - 6x + 12 = 28 \rightarrow -6x + 22 = 28$$
$$\rightarrow -6x = 6 \rightarrow x = -1$$

43) Choice B is correct

$20 - 11.49 = \$8.51$

44) Choice D is correct

Write the equation and solve for B: $0.90A = 0.30B$, divide both sides by 0.30, then you will have $\frac{0.90}{0.30}A = B$, therefore: $B = 3A$, and B is 3 times of A or it's 300% of A.

45) Choice A is correct

The probability of choosing a Hearts is $\frac{13}{52} = \frac{1}{4}$

46) Choice C is correct

$$\frac{3}{5} + \frac{\frac{-2}{5}}{\frac{4}{10}} = \frac{3}{5} + \frac{(-2) \times 10}{5 \times 4} = \frac{3}{5} + \frac{-20}{20} = \frac{3}{5} - 1 = \frac{3-5}{5} = -\frac{2}{5}$$

47) Choice B is correct

$$\frac{7 \times 15}{60} = \frac{105}{60} = 1.75 \cong 1.8$$

ISEE Middle Level Math Practice Test 4 Section 1

1) Choice B is correct

Number of visiting fans: $\frac{2 \times 25{,}000}{5} = 10{,}000$

2) Choice B is correct

In triangles sum of all angles equal to $180°$, then:$y = 180° - (100° + 28.5°) =$

$100° - 128.5° = 51.5°$

3) Choice B is correct

$\frac{2}{3} \cong 0.67$ $\frac{5}{7} \cong 0.71$ $\frac{8}{11} \cong 0.72$ $\frac{3}{4} = 0.75$

4) Choice D is correct

One hour equal to 60 minutes then, 4 hours$= 4 \times 60 = 240$ minutes

One minute equal to 60 seconds then, 240 minutes$= 240 \times 60 = 14{,}400$ seconds

Distance that travel by object is: $0.3 \times 14{,}400 = 4{,}320\ cm = 43.2\ m$

5) Choice A is correct

$243 = 3^5 \rightarrow \frac{3^x}{9} = 3^5 \rightarrow \frac{3^x}{3^2} = 3^5 \rightarrow 3^{x-2} = 3^5 \rightarrow x - 2 = 5 \rightarrow x = 7$

6) Choice B is correct

40% off is: 40% of $\$40 = \frac{40}{100} \times 40 = \$16$, then, the sales price of the sweater is $\$24$.

5% of $\$24 = \frac{5}{100} \times 24 = \$1.20$. Ava pays: $\$24 + \$1.2 = \$25.20$

7) Choice A is correct

20% of $300 = \frac{20}{100} \times 300 = 60$, Final sale price is: $300 - 60 = \$240$

8) Choice A is correct

Circumference of circle$= 2\pi r = 2\pi \times \frac{15}{2} = 15\pi = 15 \times 3.14 = 47.1\ m$

9) Choice D is correct

Area of circle with diameter 12 is: $\pi r^2 = \pi \left(\frac{12}{2}\right)^2 = 36\pi$, the area of shaded region is: $\frac{36\pi}{4} = 9\pi$

10) Choice C is correct

The amount of petrol consumed after x hours is: $6x$, Petrol remaining: $80 - 6x$

11) Choice D is correct

To find the discount, multiply the number by $(100\% - \mathit{rate\ of\ discount})$.

Therefore, for the first discount we get: (200) (100% – 15%) = (200) (0.85)

For the next 15% discount: (200) (0.85) (0.85)

12) Choice A is correct

$\frac{3}{4}$ of $290 = \frac{3}{4} \times 300 = 225$, $\frac{2}{5}$ of $225 = \frac{2}{5} \times 225 = 90$, $\frac{1}{3}$ of $90 = \frac{1}{3} \times 90 = 30$

13) Choice B is correct

$7 + 2x \leq 15 \rightarrow 2x \leq 15 - 7 \rightarrow 2x \leq 8 \rightarrow x \leq \frac{8}{2} \rightarrow x \leq 4,$ Then: $a = 4$

14) Choice A is correct

The area of trapezoid is: $\left(\frac{15+18}{2}\right) x = 132 \rightarrow 16.5x = 132 \rightarrow x = 8$

15) Choice C is correct

$3 + x + 6\left(\frac{x}{2}\right) = 2x + 10 \rightarrow 3 + x + 3x = 2x + 10 \rightarrow 2x = 7 \rightarrow x = \frac{7}{2}$

16) Choice A is correct

$One\ liter = 1{,}000\ cm^3 \rightarrow 6\ liters = 6{,}000\ cm^3$, $6{,}000 = 15 \times 5 \times h \rightarrow h = \frac{6{,}000}{75} = 80\ cm$

17) Choice C is correct

$3f + 2g = 3x + y \rightarrow 3f + 2(2y - 3x) = 3x + y \rightarrow 3f + 4y - 6x = 3x + y \rightarrow$

$3f = 9x - 3y \rightarrow f = 3x - y$

18) Choice B is correct

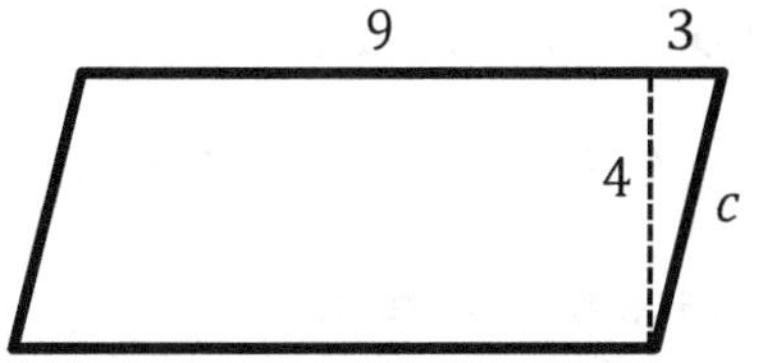

$c = \sqrt{4^2 + 3^2} = \sqrt{25} = 5$

Perimeter of parallelogram= $(9 + 3 + 5) \times 2 = 34$

19) Choice C is correct

$\frac{8}{40} \times 100 = \frac{8}{4} \times 10 = 20\%$

20) Choice A is correct

$$\frac{-\frac{11}{2} \times \frac{3}{5}}{\frac{11}{30}} = -\frac{\frac{11 \times 3}{2 \times 5}}{\frac{11}{30}} = -\frac{\frac{33}{10}}{\frac{11}{30}} = -\frac{33 \times 30}{11 \times 10} = -9$$

21) Choice D is correct

$$Average = \frac{sum\ of\ terms}{number\ of\ terms} \Rightarrow 18 = \frac{13 + 15 + 20 + x}{4} \Rightarrow 72 = 48 + x \Rightarrow x = 24$$

22) Choice B is correct

Write the numbers in order: 1, 1, 1, 2, 2, 3, 3, 3, 4, 4, 5

The mode of numbers is: 1 and 3 median is: 3

23) Choice D is correct

Let x be the integer. Then: $2x - 5 = 83$, Add 5 both sides: $2x = 88$, Divide both sides by 2:

$$x = 44$$

24) Choice C is correct

$\frac{0.25}{7.5} \times 100 = 3.33$

25) Choice C is correct

Plug in 104 for F and then solve for C. $C = \frac{5}{9}(F - 32) \Rightarrow C = \frac{5}{9}(104 - 32) \Rightarrow$

$$C = \frac{5}{9}(72) = 40$$

26) Choice C is correct

Column A: 9% of the computer cost is 24.3: $9\% \times 270 = 0.09 \times 270 = 24.3$

Column B: 24.3

27) Choice B is correct.

Column A: $3^2 - 5^4 = 9 - 625 = -616$, Column B: $3^4 - 5^2 = 81 - 25 = 56$

28) Choice B is correct.

$$3x^4 - 45 = 723 \rightarrow 3x^4 = 723 + 45 = 768 \rightarrow x^4 = \frac{768}{3} = 256 \rightarrow x = \sqrt[4]{256} = \sqrt[4]{4^4} = 4$$

$\frac{1}{5}y - \frac{4}{10} = \frac{3}{5} \rightarrow \frac{y}{5} = \frac{3}{5} + \frac{4}{10} = \frac{6+3}{10} = \frac{10}{10} = 1 \rightarrow y = 5 \times 1 = 5$

29) Choice A is correct.

Column A: Simplify. $\frac{\sqrt{81-49}}{\sqrt{16-9}} = \frac{\sqrt{32}}{\sqrt{7}} = \sqrt{\frac{32}{7}}$ which is bigger than 2 ($\sqrt{4} = 2$ and $\frac{32}{7}$ is bigger than 4). Column B: $\frac{(9-7)}{(4-3)} = \frac{2}{1} = 2$

30) Choice B is correct.

Column B: Simplify. $\sqrt{25 - 9} = \sqrt{16} = 4$

Column A: $\sqrt{25} - \sqrt{9} = 5 - 3 = 2$, $\sqrt{14}$ is bigger than 2. ($\sqrt{4} = 2$)

31) Choice B is correct.

Column A: First, find the integers. Let x be the smallest integer. Then the integers are x, $(x + 1)$, and $(x + 2)$. The sum of the integers is 54. Then:

$x + x + 1 + x + 2 = 54 \rightarrow 3x + 3 = 54 \rightarrow 3x = 51 \rightarrow x = 17$. The smallest integer is 17, therefore, the largest integer is 19 which is less than 20.

32) Choice C is correct.

Column A: Write the equation in slope intercept form. $-4x + 4y = 1 \rightarrow 4y = 4x + 1 \rightarrow$

$$y = x + \frac{1}{4}$$

Column B: The slope of the line that passes through points $(1, 3)$ and $(3, 5)$:

Use slope formula: $slope\ of\ a\ line = \frac{y_2 - y_1}{x_2 - x_1} = \frac{5-3}{3-1} = 1$

33) Choice B is correct

$10\%\ of\ x = 8\%$ of $y \rightarrow 0.1\,x = 0.08\,y \rightarrow x = \frac{0.08}{0.1}y \rightarrow x = \frac{8}{10}y$, therefore, y is bigger than x.

34) Choice B is correct

Quantity A: $(-4)^3 = (-4) \times (-4) \times (-4) = -64$, Quantity B: $4 \times 4 \times 4 = 64$

Quantity B is greater.

35) Choice C is correct

Prime factoring of 22 is: 2×11, prime factoring of 32 is: $2 \times 2 \times 2 \times 2 \times 2$

Quantity A $= 2$ and Quantity B $= 2$

36) Choice C is correct.

Use exponent "product rule": $x^n \times x^m = x^{n+m}$, Quantity A: $(1.25)^2(1.25)^6 = (1.25)^{2+6} = (1.25)^8$, Quantity B: $(1.25)^8$, The two quantities are equal.

37) Choice D is correct.

Plug in different values for x and check quantity A and B. Let's choose 1 for x. Then:

Quantity A: $x^6 = 1^6 = 1$ Quantity B: $x^{11} = 1^{11} = 1$

Now, let's choose 2 for x. Then: $2^6 < 2^{11}$

The relationship cannot be determined from the information given

ISEE Middle Level Math Practice Test 4 Section 2

1) Choice C is correct

Prime factorizing of $30 = 2 \times 3 \times 5$, Prime factorizing of $35 = 5 \times 7$

$x = LCM = 2 \times 3 \times 5 \times 7 = 210, \frac{210}{2} + 1 = 105 + 1 = 106$

2) Choice B is correct

$3^x - 15 = 66 \rightarrow 3^x = 66 + 15 = 81$ and $81 = 3^4, 3^x = 3^4 \rightarrow x = 4$

3) Choice A is correct

10 cubed is: $10^3 = 1{,}000$

4) Choice D is correct

All angles in a parallelogram sum up to 360 degrees. Since, we only have 3 angles, therefore the answer cannot be determined.

5) Choice A is correct

Swing moves once from point A to point B and returns to point A is: $30 + 30 = 60$ *seconds*

Therefore, for ten times: $10 \times 60 = 600$ seconds

6) Choice C is correct

$1\frac{2}{5} = \frac{7}{5} = 1.4$, Speed of the blue car: $1.4 \times 50 = 70$, Difference of the cars' speed:

$70 - 50 = 20$, The red car is $10\ km$ ahead of a blue car. Therefore, it takes the blue car 30 minutes to catch the red car. $\frac{10}{20} = 0.5$ Hour $= 30$ minutes

7) Choice B is correct

$y = \sqrt{3^2 + 4^2} = 5$, Perimeter is: $12 + 3 + 8 + 5 = 28$

8) Choice C is correct

The population is increased by 15% and 20%. 15% increase changes the population to 115% of original population. For the second increase, multiply the result by 120%.

$(1.15) \times (1.20) = 1.38 = 138\%$, 38 percent of the population is increased after two years.

9) Choice A is correct

Let x be the number of years. Therefore, \$2,000 per year equals $2{,}000x$. starting from \$24,000 annual salary means you should add that amount to $2{,}000x$. Income more than that is: $I > 2{,}000\,x + 24{,}000$

10) Choice D is correct

Angle between 90° and 180° is called obtuse angle.

11) Choice C is correct

Use PEMDAS (order of operation):

$$8 + 7 \times (-2) - [5 + 22 \times 4] \div 6 = 8 + 7 \times (-2) - [5 + 88] \div 6$$
$$= 8 + 7 \times (-2) - [93] \div 6 = 8 + (-14) - 15.5 = 8 + (-14) - 15.5$$
$$= -6 - 15.5 = -21.5$$

12) Choice B is correct

Perimeter $A = 4 \times 4 = 16$, Area $B = 2 \times 3 = 6$, $\frac{16}{6} = \frac{8}{3}$

13) Choice A is correct

2,500 out of 55,000 equals to $\frac{2,500}{55,000} = \frac{25}{550} = \frac{1}{22}$

14) Choice B is correct

$$Probability = \frac{number\ of\ desired\ outcomes}{number\ of\ total\ outcomes} = \frac{18}{12+18+18+24} = \frac{18}{72} = \frac{1}{4}$$

15) Choice C is correct

The area of rectangle is: $9 \times 4 = 36\ cm^2$, The area of circle is: $\pi r^2 = \pi \times (\frac{10}{2})^2 = 3 \times 25 = 75$, Difference in area is: $75 - 36 = 39$

16) Choice B is correct

$x^2 + 4x + 4 = (x + 2)^2 \rightarrow (x + 2)^2 = 100 \rightarrow x + 2 = 10 \rightarrow x = 8\ or\ x + 2 = -10 \rightarrow x = -12$

17) Choice C is correct

Only choice C is equal to 120.

$$\left(\left(\frac{30}{4} + \frac{13}{2}\right) \times 7\right) - \frac{11}{2} + \frac{110}{4} = \left(\left(\frac{30 + 26}{4}\right) \times 7\right) - \frac{11}{2} + \frac{55}{2} = \left(\left(\frac{56}{4}\right) \times 7\right) + \frac{55 - 11}{2}$$
$$= (14 \times 7) + \frac{44}{2} = 98 + 22 = 120$$

18) Choice A is correct

$$\frac{15 \times 21}{8} = \frac{315}{8} = 39.375 \sim 39.4$$

19) Choice A is correct

Let x be the number, then:

$x^2 + 10 = 35 \rightarrow x^2 = 25 \rightarrow x^2 - 25 = 0 \rightarrow (x + 5)(x - 5) = 0 \rightarrow x = 5\ or\ x = -5$

20) Choice D is correct

4.5% of $\$1{,}000 = \frac{4.5}{100} \times 1{,}000 = \$45$. For two years the interest in \$90.

21) Choice A is correct

To find the number of possible outfit combinations, multiply number of options for each factor: $6 \times 3 \times 5 = 90$

22) Choice A is correct

$$\frac{x}{8} + \frac{5}{8} = \frac{15}{4} \rightarrow \frac{x}{8} = \frac{15}{4} - \frac{5}{8} = \frac{30-5}{8} = \frac{25}{8} = \rightarrow x = 25$$

23) Choice D is correct

$|6 - 9| = |-3| = 3$

24) Choice B is correct

$y = 4ab + 3b^3$, Plug in the values of a and b in the equation: $a = 2$ and $b = 3$

$y = 4\,(2)\,(3) + 3\,(3)^3 = 24 + 3(27) = 24 + 81 = 105$

25) Choice C is correct

All three angles in a triangle add up to 180 degrees. Only choice C represents three angles of a triangle.

26) Choice C is correct

$$x + 3x - 10 = \left(2 \times \left(\frac{3}{2}x + y\right)\right) - 15 \rightarrow 4x - 10 = \left(2 \times \frac{3}{2}x\right) + 2y - 15 \rightarrow 4x - 10$$
$$= 3x + 2y - 15 \rightarrow 4x - 3x - 2y = 10 - 15 \rightarrow x - 2y = -5$$

27) Choice A is correct

Let x be price of one-kilogram of banana and y be price of one-kilogram of grape, then: $x = 2y$

$$2x + 3y = 28 \rightarrow 2(2y) + 3y = 28 \rightarrow 7y = 28 \rightarrow y = \frac{28}{7} = 4 \rightarrow x = 2 \times 4 = 8$$

28) Choice D is correct

121 is not prime number, it is divided by 11.

29) Choice B is correct

The area of the floor is: $6\ cm \times 24\ cm = 144\ cm^2$, The number is tiles needed $= 144 \div 8 = 18$

30) Choice A is correct

Weight of the blue book$= \frac{80}{0.4} = 200\ g,$ Weight of the white book$= \frac{200}{1.25} = 160\ g$

Weight of all three books: $80 + 200 + 160 = 400g$

31) Choice D is correct

Since, each of the x students in a team may invite up to 5 friends, the maximum number of people in the party is 6 times x or $6x$. $(one\ student + 5\ friends\ =\ 6\ people)$

32) Choice C is correct

Perimeter= $2\pi r = 2 \times \pi \times \frac{20}{2} = 20 \approx 62.8 \approx 63$

33) Choice B is correct

$$60\ minutes\ = 1 Hours \rightarrow \frac{270}{60} = 4.5\ hours$$

34) Choice D is correct

$180° - 35° = 145°$

35) Choice C is correct

$$\left(\left((-25) + 50\right) \times \frac{1}{5}\right) + (-10) = \left((25) \times \frac{1}{5}\right) - 10 = 5 - 10 = -5$$

36) Choice B is correct

Average speed: $\frac{340}{8} = 42.5$ miles per hour

37) Choice B is correct

Let x be the price that third person has to pay then; $56 = 8.5 + (2 \times 8.5) + x \rightarrow$

$x = 56 - 25.5 = 30.5$

38) Choice D is correct

$218{,}210 = 2.1821 \times 10^5$

39) Choice B is correct

$c = \sqrt{5^2 + 12^2} = \sqrt{169} = 13$, Perimeter is: $5 + 12 + 13 = 30$

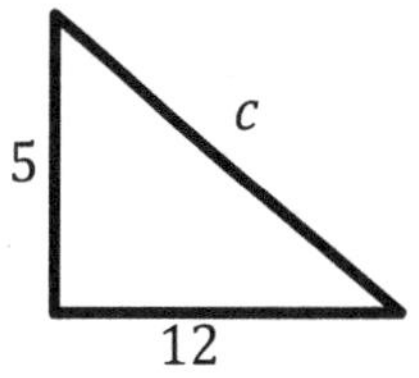

40) Choice B is correct

Let x be the number then, 120% of $x = 1.2x$, $1.2x = 0.25 \times 90 = 22.5 \rightarrow x = \frac{22.5}{1.2} = 18.75$

41) Choice B is correct

$(12 - 8)! = 4! = 4 \times 3 \times 2 \times 1 = 24$

42) Choice A is correct

The greatest even multiple odd 11 less than 80 is 66 (number 77 is odd) and the least odd multiple of 9 greater than 30 is 45. Then: $x + y = 66 + 45 = 111$

43) Choice A is correct

$average = \frac{sum\ of\ terms}{number\ of\ terms}$, The sum of the weight of all girls is: $20 \times 50 = 1{,}000\ kg$

The sum of the weight of all boys is: $30 \times 60 = 1{,}800\ kg$, The sum of the weight of all students is: $1{,}000 + 1{,}800 = 2{,}800\ kg$, $Average = \frac{2{,}800}{50} = 56$

44) Choice B is correct

Use Pythagorean Theorem: $x^2 + 15^2 = 25^2 \rightarrow x^2 = 25^2 - 15^2 \rightarrow x = \sqrt{25^2 - 15^2} \rightarrow$

$$x = \sqrt{625 - 225} = \sqrt{400} = 20$$

45) Choice C is correct

The average speed of john is: $150 \div 6 = 25$, The average speed of Alice is: $180 \div 4 = 45$

Write the ratio and simplify. $25:45 \Rightarrow 5:9$

46) Choice B is correct

The sum of supplement angles is 180. Let x be that angle. Therefore, $x + 5x = 180$, $6x = 180$, divide both sides by 6: $x = 30$

47) Choice D is correct

Smallest 4–digit number is 1,000, and biggest 4–digit number is 9,999. The difference is: 8,999

ISEE Middle Level Practice Test 5 Section 1

1) Choice C is correct

$\frac{1}{6} \cong 0.16$ $\frac{1}{3} \cong 0.33$ $\frac{2}{5} = 0.4$ $\frac{3}{4} = 0.75$

2) Choice B is correct

$$452{,}357{,}841 \times \frac{1}{10{,}000} = 45{,}235.7841$$

3) Choice C is correct

20% off equals \$23. Let x be the original price of the table. Then:

$20\%\ of\ x = 23 \rightarrow 0.2x = 23 \rightarrow x = \frac{23}{0.2} = 115$

4) Choice B is correct

Use the formula for Percent of Change: $\frac{\text{New Value} - \text{Old Value}}{Old\ Value} \times 100\%$

$\frac{28-40}{40} \times 100\% = -30\%$ (negative sign here means that the new price is less than old price)

5) Choice C is correct

$2f = 2 \times (2x - 3y) = 4x - 6y,\ 2f + g = 4x - 6y + x + 4y = 5x - 2y$

6) Choice B is correct

$$\frac{-58 \times 0.5}{4} = -\frac{58 \times \frac{1}{2}}{4} = -\frac{\frac{58}{2}}{4} = -\frac{58}{8} = -7.25$$

7) Choice D is correct

$8^x = 512 \rightarrow 8^x = 8^3 \rightarrow x = 3$

8) Choice A is correct

If the score of Mia was 60, therefore the score of Ava is 30. Since, the score of Emma was half as that of Ava, therefore, the score of Emma is 15.

9) Choice B is correct

Use the formula of areas of circles. $Area\ of\ a\ circle = \pi r^2 \Rightarrow 64\pi = \pi r^2 \Rightarrow 64 = r^2 \Rightarrow r = 8$, Radius of the circle is 8. Now, use the circumference formula: Circumference $= 2\pi r = 2\pi\,(8) = 16\pi$

10) Choice D is correct

$1.12 = \frac{112}{100}$ and $7.2 = \frac{72}{10}$ $\rightarrow 1.12 \times 7.2 = \frac{112}{100} \times \frac{72}{10} = \frac{8{,}064}{1{,}000} = 8.064 \cong 8.1$

11) Choice D is correct

Supplementary angles sum up to 180 degrees. x and 25 degrees are supplementary angles. Then: $x = 180° - 25° = 155°$

12) Choice D is correct

Let x be the number. Write the equation and solve for x. $\frac{2}{3} \times 18 = \frac{2}{5} \times x \Rightarrow \frac{2 \times 18}{3} = \frac{2x}{5}$, use cross multiplication to solve for x. $5 \times 36 = 2x \times 3 \Rightarrow 180 = 6x \Rightarrow x = 30$

13) Choice C is correct

Add the first 5 numbers. $40 + 45 + 50 + 35 + 65 = 235$

To find the distance traveled in the next 5 hours, multiply the average by number of hours.

$Distance = Average \times Rate = 50 \times 5 = 250$, Add both numbers. $250 + 235 = 485$

14) Choice D is correct

$$Mean = \frac{9 + 12 + 29 + 36 + 45 + 63 + 99 + 123}{8} = \frac{416}{8} = 52$$

15) Choice D is correct

The perimeter of the trapezoid is 60.

Therefore, the missing side (height) is = $60 - 18 - 12 - 14 = 16$

Area of the trapezoid: $A = \frac{1}{2} h (b_1 + b_2) = \frac{1}{2} (16) (12 + 14) = 208$

16) Choice D is correct

Let x be the original price. If the price of a laptop is decreased by 10% to \$360, then: 90% of $x = 360 \Rightarrow 0.90x = 360 \Rightarrow x = 360 \div 0.90 = 400$

17) Choice B is correct

$\frac{2}{5}$ of $120 = \frac{2}{5} \times 120 = 48$, $\frac{1}{4}$ of $48 = \frac{1}{4} \times 48 = 12$

18) Choice C is correct

The ratio of boy to girls is $4:7$. Therefore, there are 4 boys out of 11 students. To find the answer, first divide the total number of students by 11, then multiply the result by 4.

$66 \div 11 = 6 \Rightarrow 6 \times 4 = 24$, There are 24 boys and 42 $(66 - 24)$ girls. So, 18 more boys should be enrolled to make the ratio $1:1$

19) Choice B is correct

Simplify: $5(x + 1) = 15(x - 4) + 25$, $5x + 5 = 15x - 60 + 25$, $5x + 5 = 15x - 35$, Subtract $5x$ from both sides: $5 = 10x - 35$, Add 5 to both sides: $40 = 10x$, $4 = x$

20) Choice C is correct

Let x be the sales profit. Then, 2% of sales profit is $0.02x$. Employee's revenue: $0.02x + 5{,}000$

21) Choice D is correct

Let's review the choices:

A. $\frac{3}{4} > 0.8$ This is not a correct statement. Because $\frac{3}{4} = 0.75$ and it's less than 0.8.

B. $10\% = \frac{2}{5}$ This is not a correct statement. Because $10\% = 0.1$ and $\frac{2}{5} = 0.4$

C. $3 < \frac{5}{2}$ This is not a correct statement. Because $\frac{5}{2} = 2.5$ and it's less than 3.

D. $\frac{5}{6} > 0.8$ This is a correct statement. $\frac{5}{6} = 0.83 \rightarrow 0.8 < \frac{5}{6}$

22) Choice B is correct

$x = 20 + 125 = 145$

23) Choice B is correct

The diagonal of the square is 8. Let x be the side.

Use Pythagorean Theorem: $a^2 + b^2 = c^2$

$x^2 + x^2 = 8^2 \Rightarrow 2x^2 = 8^2 \Rightarrow 2x^2 = 64 \Rightarrow x^2 = 32 \Rightarrow x = \sqrt{32}$

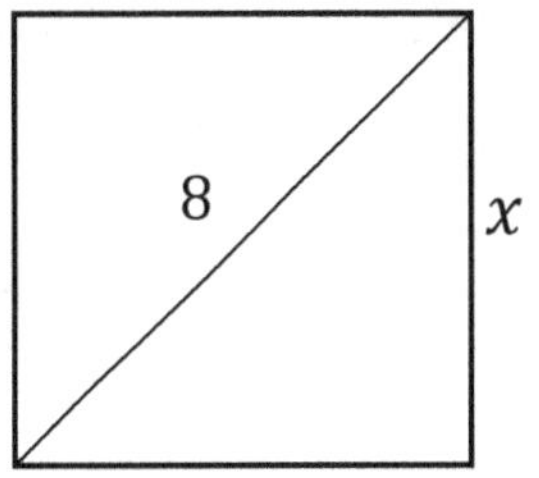

The area of the square is: $\sqrt{32} \times \sqrt{32} = 32$

24) Choice A is correct

$-26 - (-65) = -26 + 65 = 65 - 26 = 39$

25) Choice A is correct

Petrol of car A in $250km = \frac{8\times250}{100} = 20$, Petrol of car B in $250km = \frac{6\times250}{100} = 15$, $20 - 15 = 5$

26) Choice A is correct.

Column A: Use order of operation to calculate the result.

$6 + 4 \times 7 + 8 = 6 + 28 + 8 = 42$

Column B: $4 + 6 \times 7 - 8 \rightarrow 4 + 42 - 8 = 38$

27) Choice B is correct.

Column A: The value of x when $y = 12$:

$y = -4x - 8 \rightarrow 12 = -4x - 8 \rightarrow -4x = 20 \rightarrow x = -5$

Column B: -4 $\quad -4$ is greater than -5.

28) Choice A is correct.

Column A: Simplify.

$\sqrt{36} + \sqrt{36} = 6 + 6 = 12$

12 is greater than $\sqrt{72}$. ($\sqrt{144} = 12$)

29) Choice D is correct.

Column A: Based on information provided, we cannot find the average age of Joe and Michelle or average age of Michelle and Nicole.

30) Choice A is correct.

Column A: Simplify.$\sqrt{121-64} = \sqrt{57}$

Column B: $\sqrt{121} - \sqrt{64} = 11 - 8 = 3$, $\sqrt{57}$ is bigger than 3. ($\sqrt{9} = 3$)

31) Choice A is correct

Volume of a right cylinder = $\pi r^2 h \to 160\pi = \pi r^2 h = \pi(4)^2 h \to 16\pi h = 160\pi \to h = 10$, The height of the cylinder is 10inches which is bigger than 9.8 inches.

32) Choice D is correct.

Choose different values for x and find the value of quantity A.

$x = 1$, then:

Quantity A: $\frac{1}{x} + x = \frac{1}{1} + 1 = 2$

Quantity B is greater

$x = 10$, then: Quantity A: $\frac{1}{x} + x = \frac{1}{10} + 10 = 10\frac{1}{10}$. So, Quantity A is greater.

The relationship cannot be determined from the information given.

33) Choice D is correct.

Simply change the fractions to decimals. $\frac{4}{5} = 0.80, \frac{6}{7} = 0.857 \ldots, \frac{5}{6} = 0.8333 \ldots$

As you can see, x lies between 0.80 and 0.857... and it can be 0.81 or 0.84. The first one is less than 0.833... and the second one is greater than 0.833... . The relationship cannot be determined from the information given.

34) Choice A is correct.

Simplify quantity B. Quantity B: $(\frac{x}{6})^6 = \frac{x^6}{6^6}$

Since, the two quantities have the same numerator (x^6) and the denominator in quantity B is bigger ($6^6 > 6$), then the quantity A is greater.

35) Choice A is correct

Quantity A: If there are 13 marbles in the basket, 3 of them are blue. Therefore, quantity A is 6 and quantity B is 5. If you choose other values for the blue and black marbles, you will get the same result.

36) Choice C is correct

Choose different values for a and b and find the values of quantity A and quantity B.

$a = 2$ and $b = 3$, then:

Quantity A: $|2 - 3| = |-1| = 1$

Quantity B: $|3 - 2| = |1| = 1$

The two quantities are equal.$a = -3$ and $b = 2$, then:

Quantity A: $|-3 - 2| = |-5| = 5$

Quantity B: $|2 - (-3)| = |2 + 3| = 5$

The two quantities are equal. Any other values of a and b provide the same answer.

37) Choice A is correct

$$2x^3 + 10 = 64 \rightarrow 2x^3 = 64 - 10 = 54 \rightarrow x^3 = \frac{54}{2} = 27 \rightarrow x = \sqrt[3]{27} = \sqrt[3]{3^3} = 3$$

$$120 - 18y = 84 \rightarrow -18y = 84 - 120 = -36 \rightarrow y = \frac{-36}{-18} = 2$$

ISEE Middle Level Math Practice Test 5 Section 2

1) Choice B is correct

15% of $180 = \frac{15}{100} \times 180 = 27$, Let x be the number then, $x = 27 + 12 = 39$

2) Choice B is correct

Number of red cars to blue cars in a parking lot is in the ratio of $2:5$ and 90 blue cars are in the parking lot. Write a proportion and solve: $\frac{2}{5} = \frac{x}{90} \rightarrow x = \frac{2 \times 90}{5} = 36$

3) Choice B is correct

$$3 \times \left(\frac{1}{3} - \frac{1}{9}\right) + 1 = 3 \times \left(\frac{3-1}{9}\right) + 1 = \frac{6}{9} + 1 = \frac{2}{3} + 1 = \frac{5}{3} = 1.66$$

4) Choice D is correct

Number of blue pencils $= 90 - 43 = 47$, Percent of blue pencils is: $\frac{47}{90} \times 100 = 52.2\% \approx 52\%$

5) Choice B is correct

$(x + 5)^2 = 144 \rightarrow x + 5 = \sqrt[2]{144} = \sqrt[2]{12^2} = 12 \rightarrow x = 12 - 5 = 7$ or $x + 5 = -12 \rightarrow$
$x = -17$

6) Choice B is correct

50% of 36 is: $\frac{50}{100} \times 36 = \frac{36}{2} = 18$, Let x be the number then: $x = 18 - 7 = 11$

7) Choice A is correct

The perimeter of rectangle is: $2 \times (4 + 7) = 2 \times 11 = 22$, The perimeter of circle is: $2\pi r = 2 \times 3 \times \frac{10}{2} = 30$, Difference in perimeter is: $30 - 22 = 8$

Let's simplify the equation:

$x = \frac{2y}{3} - 6$, multiply both sides of the equation by 3. Then: $x = \frac{2y}{3} - 6 \rightarrow 3x = 2y - 18$, subtract $3x$ from both sides: $3x - 3x = 2y - 3x - 18 \rightarrow 2y - 3x - 18 = 0$

All other choices are not equal to the equation provided.

8) Choice B is correct

Use this formula: Percent of Change $= \frac{New\ Value - Old\ Value}{Old\ Value} \times 100\%$

$\frac{16{,}000 - 20{,}000}{20{,}000} \times 100\% = -20\%$ and $\frac{12{,}800 - 16{,}000}{16{,}000} \times 100\% = -20\%$ (negative sign simply means the value of the car decreases)

9) Choice C is correct

Let x be the number. Write the equation and solve for x. $(24 - x) \div x = 3$, Multiply both sides by x. $(24 - x) = 3x$, then add x both sides. $24 = 4x$, now divide both sides by $4.\ x = 6$

10) Choice B is correct

Only choice B is correct. $\left(\frac{10}{3} \times 27\right) + \left(\frac{5}{2} \times 2\right) = 90 + 5 = 95$

11) Choice A is correct

If $\frac{3x}{2} = 60$, then $3x = 120 \rightarrow x = 40$, $\frac{2x}{5} = \frac{2 \times 40}{5} = \frac{80}{5} = 16$

12) Choice C is correct

$\frac{1}{3} = 0.33$ $\quad \frac{7}{9} = 0.77$ $\quad 85\% = 0.85$

13) Choice B is correct

$Surface\ Area\ of\ a\ cube = 6s^2 = 150 \rightarrow s^2 = \frac{150}{6} = 25 \rightarrow s = 5$. One side of the cube is $5\ cm$. Then, the volume of the cube is: $Volume\ of\ a\ cube = s^3 = 5^3 = 125\ cm^3$

14) Choice A is correct

First, find the number. Let x be the number. Write the equation and solve for x. 150% of a number is 60, then: $1.5 \times x = 60 \Rightarrow x = 60 \div 1.5 = 40$, 90% of 40 is: $0.9 \times 40 = 36$

15) Choice D is correct

Find the difference of each pairs of numbers: $2, 3, 5, 8, 12, 17, 23, \_\_, 38$

The difference of 2 and 3 is 1, 3 and 5 is 2, 5 and 8 is 3, 8 and 12 is 4, 12 and 17 is 5, 17 and 23 is 6, 23 and next number should be 7. The number is $23 + 7 = 30$

16) Choice D is correct

All angles in a triangle sum up to 180 degrees. In an isosceles right triangle, there is a 90 degrees angle and two 45 degrees angles.

17) Choice C is correct

$0.45 + 0.3 + 2.6 + 2.94 = 6.29$

18) Choice D is correct

$\frac{2}{5} \times 25 = \frac{50}{5} = 10$

19) Choice C is correct.

A graph represents y as a function of x if

$x_1 = x_2 \rightarrow y_1 = y_2$

In choice C, for each x, we have two different values for y.

20) Choice A is correct

$13 < -3x - 2 < 22 \rightarrow$ Add 2 to all sides. $13 + 2 < -3x - 2 + 2 < 22 + 2$

$\rightarrow 15 < -3x < 24 \rightarrow$ Divide all sides by -3. (Remember that when you divide all sides of an inequality by a negative number, the inequality sing will be swapped. < becomes >)

$\frac{15}{-3} > \frac{-3x}{-3} > \frac{24}{-3}$. $-8 < x < -5$

21) Choice B is correct

Number of biology book: 35. Total number of books; $35 + 95 + 80 = 210$

The ratio of the number of biology books to the total number of books is: $\frac{35}{210} = \frac{1}{6}$

22) Choice B is correct

$60\ minutes = 1 Hours \rightarrow \frac{185}{60} = 3.08\ Hours$

23) Choice C is correct

First, simplify the equation: $2x - 12 + 4 = 4y \rightarrow 2x - 8 = 4y$. Subtract $2x$ from both sides of the equation: $2x - 2x - 8 = 4y - 2x \rightarrow -8 = 4y - 2x$. Divide both sides by 2. Then:

$-8 = 4y - 2x \rightarrow -4 = 2y - x$

24) Choice D is correct

57 is not prime number, it is divisible by 3 and 19.

25) Choice C is correct

The area of the square is 64 inches. Therefore, the side of the square is square root of the area. $\sqrt{64} = 8$ inches, four times the side of the square is the perimeter: $4 \times 8 = 32\ inches$

26) Choice D is correct
$12 is what percent of $48? $12 \div 48 = 0.25 = 25\%$

27) Choice B is correct

Let x be one-kilogram orange cost, then: $3x + (2 \times 4.2) = 26.4 \rightarrow 3x + 8.4 = 26.4 \rightarrow 3x = 26.4 - 8.4 \rightarrow 3x = 18 \rightarrow x = \frac{18}{3} = \$6$

28) Choice A is correct

$\left(\left((-12) + 20\right) \times 2\right) + (-15) = \left((8) \times 2\right) - 15 = 16 - 15 = 1$

29) Choice A is correct

The width of a rectangle is $4x$ and its length is $6x$. Therefore, the perimeter of the rectangle is $20x$. $Perimeter\ of\ a\ rectangle = 2(width + length) = 2(4x + 6x) = 2(10x) = 20x$

The perimeter of the rectangle is 80. Then: $20x = 80 \rightarrow x = 4$

30) Choice C is correct

The distance between Jason and Joe is 9 miles. Jason running at 5.5 miles per hour and Joe is running at the speed of 7 miles per hour. Therefore, every hour the distance is 1.5 miles less.

$9 \div 1.5 = 6$

31) Choice D is correct

Use PEMDAS (order of operation):

$$[5 \times (-14) + 8] - (-4) + [4 \times 5] \div 2 = [-70 + 8] - (-4) + [20] \div 2$$
$$= [-70 + 8] - (-4) + 10 = [-62] - (-4) + 10 = [-62] + 4 + 10 = -48$$

32) Choice A is correct

The percent of girls playing tennis is: $40\% \times 25\% = 0.40 \times 0.25 = 0.10 = 10\%$

33) Choice A is correct

There are twice as many girls as boys. Let x be the number of girls in the class. Then:

$x + 2x = 48 \rightarrow 3x = 48 \rightarrow x = 16$

34) Choice C is correct

The ratio of lions to tigers is 5 to 3 at the zoo. Therefore, total number of lions and tigers must be divisible by $8. 5 + 3 = 8$, from the numbers provided, only 98 is not divisible by 8.

35) Choice C is correct

Let x be the original price. If the price of the sofa is decreased by 25% to $\$420$, then:
$75\%\ of\ x = 420 \Rightarrow 0.75x = 420 \Rightarrow x = 420 \div 0.75 = 560$

36) Choice A is correct

Number of rotates in 12 second$= \frac{300\times12}{8} = 450$

37) Choice A is correct

$$10x = -45.5 + 15.5 = -30 \rightarrow x = \frac{-30}{10} = -3$$

38) Choice D is correct

Use formula of rectangle prism volume.

$$V = (length)\ (width)\ (height) \Rightarrow 2{,}000 = (25)\ (10)\ (height) \Rightarrow height = 2{,}000 \div 250 = 8$$

39) Choice B is correct

$1{,}269 = 6^4 \quad \rightarrow 6^x = 6^4 \rightarrow x = 4$

40) Choice B is correct

The area of trapezoid is: $\left(\frac{9+11}{2}\right) \times 5 = 50$

41) Choice D is correct

$$12.124 \div 0.002 = \frac{\frac{12{,}124}{1{,}000}}{\frac{2}{1{,}000}} = \frac{12{,}124}{2} = 6{,}062$$

42) Choice A is correct

$$10 + 4(x + 5 - 5x) = 10 + 4(-4x + 5) = 30 \rightarrow 10 - 16x + 20 = 30 \rightarrow -16x + 30 = 30 \rightarrow -16x = 0 \rightarrow x = 0$$

43) Choice B is correct

$18 - 12.49 = \$5.51$

44) Choice D is correct

Write the equation and solve for B:$0.60A = 0.20B$, divide both sides by 0.20, then you will have $\frac{0.60}{0.20}A = B$, therefore: $B = 3A$, and B is 3 times of A or it's 300% of A.

45) Choice B is correct

The probability of choosing a Hearts is $\frac{13}{52} = \frac{1}{4}$

46) Choice C is correct

$$\frac{3}{4} + \frac{\frac{-2}{5}}{\frac{4}{10}} = \frac{3}{4} + \frac{(-2) \times 10}{5 \times 4} = \frac{3}{4} + \frac{-20}{20} = \frac{3}{4} - 1 = \frac{3-4}{4} = -\frac{1}{4}$$

47) Choice B is correct

$$\frac{7 \times 12}{80} = \frac{84}{80} = 1.05 \approx 1.1$$

"Effortless Math Education" Publications

Effortless Math authors' team strives to prepare and publish the best quality ISEE Middle Level Mathematics learning resources to make learning Math easier for all. We hope that our publications help you learn Math in an effective way and prepare for the ISEE Middle Level test.

We all in Effortless Math wish you good luck and successful studies!

Effortless Math Authors

www.EffortlessMath.com

... So Much More Online!

- ✓ FREE Math lessons
- ✓ More Math learning books!
- ✓ Mathematics Worksheets
- ✓ Online Math Tutors

CPSIA information can be obtained
at www.ICGtesting.com
Printed in the USA
LVHW101928050820
662460LV00003B/312

9 781646 121397